W9-ABY-938

MEDICINE TALK

by Brad Steiger

E 98
M 4
S 73

MEDICINE TALK

a guide to
walking in balance
and surviving
on the earth mother

brad steiger

FEB 1 8 1975

DOUBLEDAY & COMPANY, INC., GARDEN CITY, NEW YORK, 1975

186352

Library of Congress Cataloging in Publication Data

Steiger, Brad.
  Medicine talk.

  1. Indians of North America—Medicine. 2. Indians of North
America—Religion and mythology. I. Title. E98.M4S73   299′.7
ISBN 0-385-08791-8
Library of Congress Catalog Card Number 74-1774

COPYRIGHT © 1975 BY BRAD STEIGER
ALL RIGHTS RESERVED
PRINTED IN THE UNITED STATES OF AMERICA
FIRST EDITION

To all the spiritual Warriors of the Rainbow.

May they conquer all barriers that block
the path to a new and glorious world
of unity, love, and understanding.

contents

MEDICINE TALK

1

medicine power
is now!

Medicine Power is very much for today; and throughout the North American continent, contemporary Amerindian shamans are emerging to offer their teachings and their tribal predictions to all those who seek a new way of going, a new understanding for the period of transition which they are convinced lies just a little way down the road on our linear time scale. The traditional Indians of many tribes are telling of the Great Purification, which will soon alter the world as we know it. There will be catastrophes, major Earth changes, a great loss of life. Those who have learned to walk in balance, those who have learned to live off the land, those who have learned how to enter the silence and strengthen themselves spiritually will be the ones best prepared to survive the death of the present world and to help build the new world that will rise from its ashes.

I consider myself truly fortunate to have been able to spend some very heavy hours with certain of the new shamans who have chosen to share their Medicine with brothers and sisters of all skin colors. Because of the importance of what these Medicine people have to say, I have chosen a format which will permit the reader vicariously to share those hours with me. It is my great wish that the reader visualize himself or herself walking at the side of Dallas Chief Eagle across the South Dakota Plains, working beside Sun Bear and the Bear Tribe members as they dry fruit for the Nevada winter, kneeling next to Twylah Nitsch as she selects water-polished stones from a spring in her very special Medicine place on the Cattaraugus Reservation in upper-state New York. I would hope that my occasional intrusions, which shall come primarily in the form of questions, will echo those that my readers might have asked had they been able to share those special moments with these very special people.

However, before we visit any of the Medicine people, it might be well to define Medicine Power by listing the elements which I feel comprise its essential vibratory forces. I intend such an analysis to be respectful and to be offered in a sincere desire to be helpful rather than blasphemous. I am certain that there will be some who may quarrel with certain of my itemizations, and I am equally certain that some may consider the very notion of attempting to define Medicine as an extremely controversial endeavor. But those Medicine people with whom I share so many of my visions have found only agreement with my analysis.

Recognizing that there are myriad differences among the various tribes in their expressions of individual ceremonies and ritual observances, herewith are those transcendental elements which I believe to be basic in every tribe's meta-physics and which blend together in some spiritually indefinable way to form Medicine Power:

1. The vision quest, with its emphasis on self-denial and spiritual discipline being extended to a lifelong pursuit of wisdom of body and soul.

2. A reliance upon one's personal visions and dreams to provide one's direction on the path of life.

3. A search for personal songs to enable one to attune oneself to the primal sound, the cosmic vibration of the Great Spirit.

4. A belief in a total partnership with the world of spirits and the ability to make personal contact with grandmothers and grandfathers who have changed planes of existence.

5. The possession of a nonlinear time sense.

6. A receptivity to the evidence that the essence of the Great Spirit may be found in everything.

7. A reverence and a passion for the Earth Mother, the awareness of one's place in the web of life, and one's responsibility toward all plant and animal life.

8. A total commitment to one's beliefs that pervades every aspect of one's life and enables one truly to walk in balance.

The Gulf Building at 1780 Bellaire Street in Denver stands with clean-lined, contemporary elegance in contrast to the rugged, sprawling majesty of the Rocky Mountains, which lie in the distance. There is an interesting kind of balance that is established whenever man sets about constructing a modern city of one million people against the panoramic backdrop of a splendid mountain range. It is a balance between the man-made, the perishable, and the naturally formed, the timeless. Because of my continuing quest for additional knowledge that will enable me to walk in better balance with the Earth Mother, my fellow man, and the Cosmos, I am compelled to notice such things.

I had come to Denver because I wished to speak at length with a friend who has established a balance which few men are able to accomplish. While holding down an executive position with one of the world's largest oil companies, De Wayne Wynn has balanced his spiritual and material lives through the practice of Amerindian Medicine Power.

Perhaps the most essential point of my book *Medicine Power* is that our Amerindian spiritual heritage is laden with insights fraught with special meaning for our new age of ever-rising awareness. The ancient metaphysical teachings and practices of our continent can soar beyond science to present modern man with a system of relevant spiritual guidance that can really work for anyone who will learn to walk in balance, to live in harmony with Nature and with the Cosmos.

De Wayne Wynn must certainly be considered an excellent case study of a person of mixed White-European and Amerindian descent who has learned how to function with enviable efficiency and success in the several worlds of Big Business-Materialism and Medicine Power-Spiritualism.

BRAD STEIGER: How were you able to get Gulf Oil interested in sponsoring a special branch to work with Amerindians?

DE WAYNE WYNN: After working with Gulf for some time, I found that more and more of our activities were centering in Indian country, particularly in the Rocky Mountains and the western states. I sent in a proposal that we do something to help the Indians, understanding that Amerindian needs and desires and cultural background were much different from any other disadvantaged groups with which we were working. Since it took someone who understood these differences, I, because I am part Cherokee, was assigned the job of setting up an office and establishing a direct line of communication between the corporation and different Indian communities.

This was really not a new thing. We have been in business with the Indian communities for years. But we feel that it is a part of our obligation as a company to redistribute the wealth of the company. We have found that establishing a direct contact with the Amerindian communities has improved our relationship with them immensely. Now they feel free to call me direct on any problems.

STEIGER: Could you name some of the projects in which you are involved at the present time?

WYNN: There is a good organization here in Denver called the Coalition of Indian Controlled School Boards, a group of people and Indian educators who have felt the need to establish a good rapport between American Indians and the educational community, especially in the lower grade levels. Most Indian kids have been educated in the Bureau of Indian Affairs schools or in schools wherein there was nothing taught about Indian culture or Indian values. The CICSB is organized to encourage all established schools in the area to teach these Indian values and the culture.

This year I have given something like twenty-five grants for Indian libraries at the grade-school level. In conjunction with this, we have also given many grants to Indian studies programs in colleges.

Rather than coming in and saying, "We are going to do

this for you," we approach the Indian and ask, "What can we do *for* you?" Because of this, our *rapport* with Indian people has been outstanding.

STEIGER: Would you grant aid to an archaeological dig?

WYNN: We have supported digs in New Mexico and Arizona.

STEIGER: You don't feel such digs may violate sacred ground?

WYNN: We don't do anything without the permission of the tribes. These digs were done by tribal archaeologists with tribal permission. All of the artifacts went into the tribal museums. We have not supported anything off reservations.

STEIGER: So everything has been done with the proper ceremonial observances.

WYNN: By all means. Medicine men are there, and everything is done very methodically. We would not support anyone desecrating a burial ground.

STEIGER: Would you sponsor an "Anglo" project?

WYNN: I would not support an Anglo getting involved in a project in the Indian community, because there are enough Indians at every step of the educational levels to staff their own projects. I would support an Anglo if he had a venture with the Indian people. We want ways of putting more Indians to work.

STEIGER: Does Gulf support any of your research with herbal medicines?

WYNN: No, that research is done strictly on my own, but I am able to do this at the same time that I am conducting business on the various reservations.

I think it is a good thing that people are becoming aware of these Indian medicines. One plant that I am extremely excited about right now is the jojoba bean, which, as far as we know, grows only on the San Carlos Apache Reservation. The Apache people have been using the bean for years, extracting the wax, and using it to cure skin cancer.

In addition to remarkable cures of skin problems, jojoba bean oil can be used to replace sperm whale oil for use in high-performance engines. The Israelis have a plant similar to the jojoba bean, and they are raising it commercially for their own uses.

We are conducting laboratory tests right now, at no cost to the San Carlos Apache. I am not at liberty to discuss these tests at this time, but we do feel the extract will be good not only for skin blemishes, and possibly skin cancer, but that it will also have many additional commercial uses.

STEIGER: In addition to compiling lists of herbal medicines, I know that you are enthusiastic about the Medicine man's function as an able psychotherapist.

WYNN: Indeed! Let me tell you about my latest visit to Phoenix. I can't mention names because the woman involved is the wife of a very prominent man who is in government.

It seems that she had suffered a nervous breakdown and had gone to many doctors who were unable to help her. Then her parents took her to Oklahoma to attend an Indian prayer meeting—which was, in this case, a peyote ceremony, which I think is a very moving ceremony.

The woman went into the meeting very disturbed, almost catatonic. At the end of the ceremony, she walked out a whole woman. She is great now. I talked to her by telephone just last week.

Such things prove to me that the Indian people have known some very important things for many years. I see no difference whether one goes to the native doctor or to the psychiatrist.

STEIGER: Do you feel she underwent some kind of catharsis during the peyote ceremony?

WYNN: She said that during the ceremony she felt that she was drawn back in time. All she heard was the drums and the chants of her people. She felt that she was reliving the experience in another lifetime. She was aware of everything that was going on around her, but she was living another life.

When the ceremony was completed, she felt as though she had walked into a new day, a new life. Her problems were gone.

She is now once again emotionally stable and taking no medication of any kind. This is a beautiful thing.

STEIGER: Would such a ceremony work for a non-Indian?

WYNN: Certainly, if he truly believed in the ceremony. I don't think one could have anything happen if he went to a ceremony and said, "This is going to cure me!" It would take someone who was really sincere in his beliefs. You have to become involved and believe in it. It works.

STEIGER: Your great-grandfather was a Medicine man.

WYNN: Yes, he was a full-blooded Cherokee shaman in Oklahoma. My father died when I was quite young, but fortunately I have some cousins living in eastern Oklahoma who are able to fill me in on great-grandfather's background.

My mother was supersensitive all of her life. My sister and brother both have what one today calls "ESP" abilities. Until recently, I just assumed everyone used these abilities. They are so natural.

STEIGER: I agree, but perhaps we are yet in a minority.

Do you ever find people in the upper echelons around here looking a bit peculiarly at you?

WYNN: They know I practice Medicine, because I make no secrets about it. I have no comments about it. The president of Gulf Oil was here Friday, and he is very much for the Indians and anything we can do for them.

I know I have something really strong. There has not been one thing denied me since I got this job.

I really wanted this position. We went to prayer meetings and we prayed for me to get such a job. It happened, and it has been wonderful.

I never wish anyone harm, but in two instances since I have been here in Denver, I have had conflicts with two top managers who downgraded the Indian people. In the back of my mind, I said, I am going to get rid of you. I did not mean through serious injury, of course; but I knew they must be removed from the scene if I were to function effectively.

Today they are both gone. They were top management personnel, but I just concentrated on the fact that they must go.

One of them wrote to me and said that it had been my fault that he had been removed. Of course, I did not have that kind of authority with the company, but there is another kind of authority.

Each of these men got another good job, so they were not harmed. I would never wish harm on anyone. It was just that their work had to terminate here.

STEIGER: What meditation techniques do you practice?

WYNN: I like to tune in with music. I turn on soft music, lie down, and close my eyes. I get good vibes, and I feel so fresh and relaxed.

I get good feelings from certain articles. For instance, this ring, which was given to me by a Navaho. I get good vibes from it. It makes me feel good.

Sometimes I use the Indian way of fire. That is what we use in the peyote ceremony. You look at the small fire, and let yourself go with the chanting and the drums.

My cousin in Arizona, who is really into Indian ways, always has a candle that he lights in a dark room for meditation. He gets renewed by doing this.

STEIGER: You are a member of the Native American Church, aren't you, De Wayne?

WYNN: Yes, I feel my needs are fulfilled by attendance in these beautiful ceremonies.

STEIGER: Why do you feel that Medicine Power is now returning with such force?

WYNN: I think one of the reasons that it is returning is because the younger Indians have felt that they have missed something. A generation or so ago, Indian people decided that they did not want their children to learn about their culture, because they did not want them to be discriminated against. But now these same people, as well as their children, have begun to feel that they have lost a great deal of their heritage.

The Indians do have a culture, a heritage that they can trace. Now they want to maintain this culture; they are rediscovering the beauty of the native American life and its religion.

At the last tribal prayer meeting of the Cheyenne, there were as many young people as there were older people. John Broken Legs, the native religious leader of the northern Cheyennes and the formal tribal chairman of the Cheyenne for the past fourteen years, was delighted. It was so wonderful to have the young people, the college kids, joining in a recognition of their Indianness.

A good example of what I am talking about is my friend Lee Cook, who is president of the National Congress of American Indians. Lee felt that his three kids were missing something, so he went to the priest of the Roman Catholic church they attended and told him that he was going to start attending the Native American Church because he wanted his children to know of its beauty. But there was nothing in the Native American Church that made him not want to be a Catholic as well. They still go to the Catholic church once a month.

The old people are rediscovering the values of their heritage, and the younger people are realizing what they are missing. Everybody is coming back. They are finding what has always been there, and they are taking pride in it.

For a while peyote was completely forbidden in ceremonies in the United States. Then about five years ago, more fair-minded laws were passed and the Peyote Church has become an open religion. It has nothing to hide from or to be ashamed of.

STEIGER: None of the primitive orgies we used to hear about during the ceremonies?

WYNN: Oh, my goodness! Only one person ever speaks at a time. All the sounds that are heard come from the singer and the drummer. I wouldn't be ashamed to take anyone to our church. I would be proud if someone would want to go.

Of course, I would not want someone to accompany me who was attending with the idea of making fun of us. Our church is a beautiful thing. People don't have to hide from this.

STEIGER: How would you answer an Indian who was just beginning to make it in Anglo society who might accuse you of reinforcing white stereotypes of the Amerindian by talking about peyote ceremonies and Medicine Power?

WYNN: Such a thing has never happened to me. There are Indian people who do not wish to participate in this and who do feel that only a minority of the Indians practice such things. Each person has to have his own individual choice. I don't think one becomes stereotyped attending the Native American Church anymore than if he belonged to any other church. If someone were to term what we do as superstition, then I suppose that same person might be predisposed to categorize all religious practice as superstitious.

STEIGER: It would appear that you function very well in the twentieth century and that you have not been inhibited in anyway by your beliefs. If anything, it seems that you feel spiritually advanced.

WYNN: Oh, indeed I do. There is just one Great Spirit, and whatever way you worship God is just between the two of you. Whether you have a prayer meeting in a teepee or in some large stone edifice, there is no difference.

In my opinion, the Indian's philosophy is so beautiful. The Indian can pause, look at the waterfall, and be moved. Every morning I am grateful. I get inspired looking at the mountains. It is the Spirit doing this. For some people this may be a problem. Not for me; I have something going.

For me, the Spirit is part of life. It is part of my heritage. It is a natural thing.

Brad, some heavy things have happened to me during church ceremonies. I seem to be somewhere else. I can close my eyes and be in another time. It is a beautiful, relaxed sensation that I get. I get rid of a lot of inner emotions and inner turmoil from business.

During two ceremonies, I have been told that I was singing with the Cheyenne in the chants. I was asked where I learned these chants, and I had to say that I know nothing of Cheyenne. I didn't even realize that I had joined the chanting. People said that the Spirit had come.

STEIGER: I have always been fascinated by your experience with that bit of pottery your cousin unearthed when he was building his new house in Arizona.

WYNN: Yes, this one particular piece of pottery gave me beautiful vibes. I still get beautiful vibes from it. Actually, the hair raises up on my arms, my neck. In fact, I feel it is part of my history, my background.

It is the most unusual piece of pottery that I have ever seen. The inside of the piece is glazed with a substance that looks like today's Teflon that is used in frying pans. Archaeologists in Arizona took some of the other pieces and said that they could cook in them without anything sticking to them. They estimate the age of the pottery at 950 to a thousand years ago. Just think, a thousand years ago, the Indians had "Teflon."

I know that particular piece of pottery has a lot of power in it for me. I like to go up to it and touch it and talk to it. That is why I keep it at home.

STEIGER: You seem to have little difficulty practicing your Medicine as you sit in a modern office in a city of a million people.

WYNN: Not at all. I think one must get away from the crowds from time to time, but I think it is very important to practice Medicine every day. It brings a power, a fulfillment, a calmness. Practice Medicine in your car, your office, your home—anywhere.

I wish that when people felt pressured or tense, they would sit quietly down and think about their own lives and what is meaningful to them. By going into the Silence, they would accept the fact that there is something to which they can reach out, something to which they can talk, something which can fulfill them—whether they call it God or the Great Spirit. People don't have to meet with a group every week. Everyone can practice Medicine on an individual basis in his daily life every day.

De Wayne Wynn is a Medicine practitioner, not a Medicine man, but the manner in which he employs his spiritual insights enables him to walk in balance in the Earth Mother in his position as a high-ranking executive of a modern industry. Although De Wayne may not be the stereotyped businessman, there is no reason why he could not serve as a model for anyone who might wish to function equally well in the seemingly disparate worlds of competitive commercialism and essential spiritualism.

2

twylah's
wisdom of the seneca

A few hours ride from the railroad station in a wagon, not the easiest, of a road, not the smoothest, meeting narrow escapes as to mudholes and deep ruts, and you will find yourself upon the Cattaraugus Indian Reservation. You might as well be west of the Rocky Mountains for any indications of the Paleface that you see here. Indians on the roads and in the homes, working on the farms and building houses; Indian children with ball-clubs, snow-snakes and arrows; Indian babies upon the backs of their mothers; Indian corn bread boiling in the kettles under the trees; Indians here, there, and everywhere, the straight black hair and shining black eyes that mark the race everywhere meet you here. You hear the curious intonations of their strange language all about you, and yet you are only 30 miles south of Buffalo, and 500 miles from New York

City. (OUR LIFE AMONG THE IROQUOIS INDIANS, *Mrs. Harriet S. Caswell,* 1892.)

Eighty-one years later than the Caswells arrived on the Cattaraugus Reservation, my wife, Marilyn, and I were entering a Seneca home that had been built long before Harriet Caswell viewed the scene she described in her book. Although Twylah Nitsch's ancestral home had been constructed after the style of the white man in 1858, each succeeding generation had contributed its own new room, new roof, or new siding. The house we entered was clean and neat, ready for the most fastidious white-glove test. Modern appliances, attractive carpeting, and a baby grand piano blended with Amerindian objects d'art and artifacts.

Twylah, smiling her welcome, eyes sparkling with insight and intelligence, had met us at the Buffalo airport. The hour's drive was filled with talk and laughter, and if we had "narrow escapes as to mudholes and deep ruts," we took no notice of them, as we gave the responsibility of the journey to the reservation over to Twylah and her Mercury Monterey.

Seldom have my wife and I discovered an individual with whom we both had instant *rapport*. Meeting Twylah had presented us with an overwhelming sensation of *déjà vu*. In some other time, some other place, forgotten—yet now strangely remembered—we had met and loved this delightful woman.

On both her grandfather's as well as her grandmother's side of the family Twylah is a descendant of the great Seneca chief Red Jacket. Red Jacket was a staunch defender of his people's traditions and a brilliant orator. Twylah has inherited both attributes.

In the Nitschs' study is a cherished portrait of Red Jacket that has been in Twylah's family for years. On the back of the portrait a stylish hand once wrote with quill pen, "Taken from life by Joseph B. Gardner of Nantucket, July 21, 1835."

Shortly after we arrived at the Nitsch home, Twylah invited us to meet a committee that had assembled in a long, low, nearby building to discuss future events of the Seneca Indian Historical Society. The building, we learned as we followed Twylah, had been the original Buffalo Creek longhouse of the Senecas. Twylah's husband, Bob, had recently remodeled the longhouse into a utilitarian studio for crafts work and classes.

Twylah, together with her mother, Maude Hurd, and three other Seneca women living on the Cattaraugus Reservation, founded the historical society early in 1970. The brief business meeting was taken up with such matters as how to obtain grants and aids, how best to conduct arts and crafts programs, and, interestingly, how to attract white people to attend functions held on the reservation. Apparently even whites in the area had little knowledge of their Amerindian neighbors' homelife, and a good many seemed to express a great reluctance, even fear, of entering the reservation.

Later, after the committee had adjourned, Twylah fixed us a light supper. Bob had to be lured into the house to take time away from his maintenance of the spacious yards surrounding the home and outbuildings. The weather, enjoyably mild for the first week in December, had grown a bit chilly while Bob trimmed the still-green grass around the large willow trees. Now the warmth of their comfortable home, together with the roast beef sandwiches, made Bob want to stretch out and watch television.

"He'll soon be watching it through the back of his head while he lies curled up on the floor," Twylah teased, as her husband excused himself.

Marilyn helped our hostess clear the table and clean the dishes, then we all knew that it was time to talk of Medicine Power, Seneca Wisdom.

"The first thing I want to ask of you, Brad, before we really get into things, is that you ask people to stop using the word 'squaw,'" Twylah said. "Do you know what 'squaw' means?"

Of course I knew that "squaw" was used in countless motion pictures and popular novels of cowboys-and-Indians fiction as the word denoting the wife of an Indian man. Since there are many diverse Amerindian languages and dialects, it is obvious that all tribes did not originally use the word "squaw" to identify the female members of their groups. No doubt the early fur traders had corrupted an eastern tribe's word for woman, and their version of the Amerindian's pronunciation had become standard and universal in its application. But I had noticed that some Amerindian women rankled at the word and seemed to consider its usage as pejorative. And Twylah's tone of voice told me that she considered the use of the word to be reprehensible.

"The word probably originally meant a beast of burden," I answered Twylah, taking what I considered to be an educated guess.

Twylah seemed amused, but she frowned and shook her head. "When the fur trappers came on their boats, they had been away from their towns for a long time, and they were looking for women. They couldn't make the Indian men understand what they wanted, so they exposed their genitals and made suggestive movements.

"The Indian men said, 'Oh, *numsquaw*,' giving the word for the male genitals. The traders brightened, thinking they had made themselves understood, and shouted, 'Yeah! Squaw! Squaw! Squaw!'

"So you see, Brad and Marilyn, Indian women don't want to be called squaws, because they have no right to the word. It has nothing to do with women. I want to get letters off to the dictionary companies, asking them to delete the word. Not to make it an issue, but just to delete squaw from the dictionary. People think it is an Indian word for woman, and it certainly is not."

Her valid social statement had now been made and duly noted, so Twylah turned to a subject very dear to her heart and spirit—her grandfather, Moses Shongo, last of the great Seneca Medicine doctors:

TWYLAH: I would like to tell you that before I was born my grandfather was very worried about who was going to take over the teachings. He had handed his Medicine bag to his son. My mother had a child who had died at birth, and it seemed that they were not going to have any more children.

Eventually, Mother became pregnant. Grandfather and Mother conducted some Indian rituals to make sure that she was in proper condition to carry this child. He would say to her, "Maybe this child will live and carry on where I have found no one else to do so."

I was born, and he said, "This child will be able to walk on two paths. She has white blood in her, as well as Indian blood; therefore, she will be able to move from the Indian to the white."

When I was about two years old, I came down with a very

serious case of whooping cough. In those days there were no effective medicines to overcome this. Even today, whooping cough is very hazardous for a young child.

One night during the course of my illness, I coughed and choked. Mother became frightened, because I was turning blue. She quickly got my grandfather (we all lived together). He used mouth-to-mouth resuscitation, and he brought me around.

He said to Mother, "Now she will carry on my work, because my breath is her breath."

My mother told me this about a year before she died. Of course, no one had heard about mouth-to-mouth resuscitation at the time, but Grandfather saved my life with it.

About six months before she died, Mother said, "I don't know why I am still around. I have taught you everything I know. I don't know what else I can do. I can help much more on the other side." I said, "Mother, you must still have something to do."

She slept upstairs. She went to bed, and suddenly at the foot of the bed, Grandpa and her brother and grandmother were standing there.

She said, "Oh, what are you here for? Did you come for me?"

They said, "No, you have to tell Twylah that it is all right. She must do the teaching and the sharing she is thinking about doing. She is not listening to us. She withdraws once it comes to the point of doing it. She has got to do it. We have given this knowledge to her, and we are helping her."

Mother came downstairs. She said, "Twy, I have to tell you what happened." She told me, and I felt so good. Mother said, "The time is now."

Just prior to Mother's dream, I would go to Rosary Hill College, where I was teaching, with the strongest feeling that I should take Grandpa's stone pestle to class. One day I took it into the house, got some Indian tobacco, ground it, and burned it.

Mother said, "You should never have done this." I said, "Mom, I had to. Grandpa impressed me to do it."

Mother was very upset with me, because she went along to class. She said, "If you do it right, it will be fine; but you have never done it!" I said I would do it right.

I conducted a very simple ceremony. I asked Mother to pray. Her prayer was beautiful. On our way home, I said, "It was all right, wasn't it?" Mother agreed that it was. That class is still talking about that ceremony!

That experience, together with Mother's dream, was all I needed. From then on, all these things have been coming to me.

Neither your mother nor your father are living today.

No, my mother passed away two years ago, and my father passed away four years ago. Mother was a very marvelous person. She had a great deal of spiritual depth. My father could have had, but he just didn't get involved in the closeness of the Indian, except to do the craft work and to help with initiations and adoptions. We have had fairs here on this farm all the time. It is a place for people to come. The name was Shongo Farms. Everyone knew the place.

What does shongo mean?

Shongo is not an Indian name per se. Shongo is a contraction, an abbreviation. It means "in the spring . . . in the water."

Years ago, the Seneca would take the newborn child, place

it in spring water to help it draw its first breath. I recall being told that when I was born and I wasn't crying, I was placed in the cold water, just enough to alarm the body.

And this is truly your ancestral home.

Yes, I was born here. My mother was born here, and I was born on my mother's birthday.

What year did your great-grandfather build the house on this farm?

Great-grandfather Two Guns started to build it in 1858. He moved in when my grandmother was a baby. When the Seneca came down here, the Deer clan lived on the other side of the road. The Wolf clan lived on this side. Bob was very perturbed because our family didn't adopt him. They didn't adopt him, because he was married to me. He would have to be adopted by another clan. The Deer clan adopted him so he could be a Deer married to a Wolf. Many Deer married Wolves. You never marry in your clan.

Jane Pierce was my grandmother. She married Daniel Webster Pierce, who taught in the district school as an educator. She was one of the students. They fell in love. He was a few years older, of course. They had just one daughter, my grandmother. The Indians called her "that white woman," because she was a descendant of Mary Jamison, an early white captive of the Senecas. Because the Indians and the white people weren't exactly on good terms, "white" was a bad word.

My Grandfather Moses Shongo came from Allegheny, from the Buffalo Creek Reservation. He came up here and married my grandmother. When there is a marriage among Seneca, the women take the husbands to their own homes. Today the life-style is somewhat the same. I did the same thing. Bob came to my home.

We came down here from Buffalo and fixed the place up. Bob didn't know at first, but when the polio epidemic came around, we wanted to get the family out of the city. It was quite a change—no electricity, no running water. Nothing but plain country living. Bob loved it so much, he said he was willing to take a stab at it.

Was there any resentment toward a whiteman living on the reservation?

My dad was considered white, because he was one-quarter Oneida. His people died when he was very young, and a white family took his sister and him into their home.

When Dad's Oneida grandmother came to visit, the white family chased her away. They called her a witch. Dad ran away, but they caught him before he could find her. He was only ten years old. When he went into the Army, he met my mother's brother, who introduced him to my mother, and they were married.

When Dad lived down here, people called him a whiteman, too. Even now if someone gets mad at me, they call me a white woman.

I don't believe there is one family on the reservation that is 100 per cent Indian.

How many Indians here on the reservation are following the traditional ways?

There are very few. They don't know the ways my grandfather taught me. Those teachings are very simple. There are four questions, which also serve as guidelines in self-discipline.

Ask yourself: 1. Am I happy in what I'm doing? 2. Is what I'm doing adding to the confusion? 3. What am I doing to bring about peace and contentment? 4. How will I be remembered when I am gone?

If you are with your friends, you ask yourself, am I happy with my friends? If there is a discussion which creates an argument, what did I do to add fuel to the fire? Was I responsible for it? What did I do to bring about peace and contentment? How will I be remembered when I am gone? These questions make a circle. You can keep on going around and around.

When disciplining a child, ask him if he is happy doing what he is doing. If he is happy doing the naughtiness, he may answer yes. Then explain to him what will happen if he continues. Let him know if he continues, he alone will be responsible. I learned a lot of lessons that way!

The Indians always believed in one Creator. The energy or the force or the power of the Creator will manifest itself in any possible way. You always pray in thanksgiving for this magnificent force. For this reason, the Indian could embrace the Christian religion. Christ taught brotherly love, and that is what this was. The Indian felt kinship to all creatures. The Indians could accept Christianity in that way.

When we went to live in the city while I was going to school, I went to every church that we were near. I have been baptized four times, because everyone wanted to save that little Indian girl.

The Indian never had any religious wars. They recognized one Supreme Force, which dwelt in the Indian and in everything.

You mentioned being baptized four times. Were you or your parents or grandparents ever members of any orthodox, mainstream church?

Oh, yes, we belonged to the Presbyterian Church. My great-grandfather embraced Christianity, and he was a min-

34

ister. He preached at the United Mission church over here. There are about fifteen different denominations on this reservation.

When the different religious sects came to this reservation, the people accepted them. The missionaries were kind people who wanted to do what they could to make the Indian adapt to the new environment in which they so suddenly found themselves.

In 1800 an Indian fellow by the name of Handsome Lake came up with his Longhouse religion. Of course it is very close to the Bible. He did a service for his people. The other churches offered nothing to the Indian that was compatible with the Indian life-style.

Handsome Lake's religion flourished for about fifteen years while he was teaching. There was a great deal of misunderstanding. It was then that there began to be arguments among Indians about religion. Prior to any other nations coming to this country, the Indians did not have a word for sin.

There was no punishment from an angry God. The Indian could not understand all the white people coming and telling him that his way of life was wrong, that he couldn't be saved, that his God couldn't do this or that.

Are you a member of an orthodox church today?

My husband is a Lutheran. When we were married I had been to so many different churches, I thought it better we go to his church. My children were baptized in the Lutheran Church.

I don't go to any church now, because there is so much politics in all the churches. I have nothing against any of the basic beliefs of the churches, because fundamentally they are the same. I believe everyone is getting to God in his own way.

35

I talk to different people who want to search me out, and I hope I can give them just a little something to think about. I hope that I can say something to give them a little more peace of mind and to help them learn a little more about themselves. I have never forced any thought on anyone.

Whenever I start to speak, I tell people that my presentation is for information only. If I should happen to have a little gift for them to receive that would enrich their lives, fine.

I surely am not going to argue with anyone. I speak of the Seneca's life-style before the whiteman came here. It is no longer in existence, because the life-style of the average Seneca today has been blended in with the American culture as much as possible.

When you were a young woman, did you have any difficulty leaving the reservation? Dallas Chief Eagle has said that growing up on a reservation is worse than growing up in a prisoner-of-war camp; because at least in a war camp, one has hope that the war will be over.

The Pine Ridge and Rosebud people have an environmental problem entirely different from ours. The Cattaraugus Indian Reservation and all the other eastern reservations are in urban areas. Our Indians have a much greater chance of using their skills.

Due to the balance of their existence with nature, Indians are experts in maintaining physical balance. You will find many of the Iroquois who are builders. As the East developed faster than the West, due to a denser population of people, the eastern Indian had a better opportunity to learn trades than did the western Indian.

Whenever I leave my home to go into the cities, I am tickled to death that I can come home to the reservation.

The minute I come over the hill, I know there is peace. We lived in the city while I went to school, and every opportunity we had, we came home. This is home.

Even if you had settled in the city, you would still come home.

You can tell by what Bob said tonight that this is home. His roots are deep in this place. I never prompted him. You can't put words in his mouth. He is devoted to this place. You heard me talking today in our business meeting about the problems we have in getting the whiteman to come to the reservation. There is a certain fear. We don't know why. There doesn't seem to be any problem with the younger generation, but their parents have a fear of coming here.

An Indian feels safe here. We walk around after dark and leave our doors open. In the city you can't walk around after dark, or you may have something happen to you. There is a different kind of feeling here. There is a spiritual peace that you cannot find in the city.

We have joined an association of all artists to cover several counties, but the white people are still reluctant to come to the reservation. They will use the excuse "I thought the craft show was just for Indians." Yet on the brochures we sent out, it is stated that the show is for everyone. Those whites who do come are delighted that they came. They are like scouts for the wagon train.

Any ideas as to why this situation exists?

It is because of the cowboy-and-Indian idea. We have people who come on the reservation and expect to find teepees. They will come down and ask, "Where are the Indians?" It is silly.

When I go out and lecture, I put on my costume and white people will say to me, "Do you ever wear any other clothes?"

37

In one instance, this woman said, "I wonder where our speaker is? They said she would be here early." I had been introduced to her, but she hadn't got my name. Finally the lady next to me said maybe I should be excused to put my costume on. I excused myself and got dressed in costume. As I walked in again, the lady said, "Oh, there she is. I was sitting across the table from her!"

I fear that our entire educational process has always portrayed the Indians as a part of America's past. The implication is that Indians don't even exist today.

It is true, Brad. The Indians of this area have lost much of their heritage. Few can speak the language, but they want to learn it. The historical society is teaching classes in Indian language.

In the past it has been better not to be identified as an Indian, because it put you in a different class right away. I know; I have been through it. I went to school that way. I was different. Every Indian goes through this.

Indians like television sets, homes, and their jobs, just like the whites do. The homes on the reservation are beginning to look like any other American homes. The Indian has an inner peace—if he has retained his Indianism. The reason some are ashamed of their Indianism is that there has been so much confusion within their own families.

Your courtship, according to your husband's testimony, had no problems due to your own Indianism.

No, not for him; but his family frowned on it. They were ashamed that their son had left the city and moved to the reservation.

But before my father-in-law died of cancer, he called me into his room. He said, "Twy, I have to tell you this. You know, when Bob married you, we were very much disappointed. A father and a mother always feel the girl their son marries is never good enough for him. I want to tell you that I can say now that I couldn't have found a better wife for my son."

I felt marvelous. All these years he had had this within his heart.

When we were married, they never asked us to the house. When our picture would be in the paper, my mother-in-law would be asked if that Indian was her daughter-in-law. Now my mother-in-law is helping me in my Indian projects. At Thanksgiving, she stayed four days. It was fun. So you see, this is the blending after all these years. It makes my husband very happy.

What about your children? Are they into Indianness?

My daughter Janice is writing Indian clan stories for small folks. The book I have written is for seventh or eighth or possibly ninth grade level. Together, we are going to put it on possibly a fifth grade level. Diane has a little bit, but she is not quite ready. She is still doing her thing. She is a speech therapist. The two boys know all the tricks of the trade and use them in everything that they do. Our older boy is a musician and musician's agent in Florida. He wears his environment [Medicine] stone all the time. He wouldn't go without it.

When he, our son Bob, was in the service—he was in the navy band—I had a vision of him on an ocean liner with sirens sounding all around him. I could see that there was trouble, but that Bob was all right if he stayed right where he was. I kept projecting to him, "Bob, you're all right. Don't move. Stay where you are!"

Weeks later I got a letter from him saying, "Mother, you were so clear. I could see you and I could hear you saying, 'Stay where you are!' "

He had listened to my image, and everything had worked out fine. They had been playing aboard an ocean liner when fire broke out. He just stayed right where he was until things were back under control.

Bob and I have a thing going. He will telephone me and ask what I want. He knows when I am thinking about him, wanting to talk to him. Both of the boys, Bob and Jim, and I speak freely of these things. Diane will intellectualize, just as her father will. Janice is pretty well into it.

Did you do anything special when they were children to encourage, or to develop, these abilities?

Yes, we meditated. I want to start working with my grandchildren in the same way. I have had them in my classes, and they say, "Grandma, when can we do these things again?"

Do you feel any link between you and your ancestor, Red Jacket?

Yes, he is with me a lot. I wasn't going to mention this, but you picked it up, I know. My grandmother and grandfather are constantly with me. My mother is, too, if I ask her to come. This is the way the Indian operates: He talks to his people in the Spirit World. I listen to what my people there tell me.

I feel that my role in this life is to help others help themselves to adapt to their environment and to find themselves so they can obtain peace of mind. If each person could obtain his own peace of mind, he would help the entire world purify itself. Each individual could help change the entire picture.

Twylah asked me if I had my Medicine stone with me. I reached into a pocket, brought forth the small, oblong stone which I carry.

"My daughter Julie gave this to me when she was four years old," I said. "She had been outside somewhere, and when she came back into the house, she presented this rather uniquely shaped stone with the announcement that it was to be mine. Since she was at that possessive-ownership age, I assumed something pretty heavy must have told her that this was to be my Medicine stone."

Twylah took my stone, held it thoughtfully in an open palm. "Yes, I am sure that this is your stone. But let us find another for both of you."

She took two rather large bags from a closet of the long-house workshop. "Here," she said, dumping their contents on the floor, "choose your stone from among these. Pass your hand over them until one sends out the vibration that it is yours."

Marilyn and I knelt, moved our hands over the stones.

"Open yourselves," Twylah admonished us. "Open up and let the stones speak to you. When you have selected a stone, I shall read it for you.

"The foundation of the universe is a stone. A stone is a common denominator of the universe. You can find one wherever you go. A stone has form and spirituality. Even the uninitiated have feelings for stones, whether they realize it or not. When this Earth is cleansed, it will be the stone that will be the nucleus and expand or contract. The Indians have a beautiful philosophy that revolves around the stone, and it has almost been lost."

"Early missionaries used to bemoan the fact that the Indians worshipped stones," I said.

Twylah smiled, shook her head slowly. Her eyes closed momentarily, as if she were visualizing a memory of a scene that had occurred before her own birth.

"The Indians did not worship the stone. The Indian used the stone to remind him of the oneness of all creatures of the universe and that the same spiritual energy flows through all things.

"Let me recite for you a poem, a song, that came to me about stones. These things come to me, Brad. First a title comes. Then I wait. The song-poem comes in spurts. Through the night, I will dream it. I am not me. I have no image. I am floating around. It is not me, Twylah, writing such things down."

THE BLESSED EVENT

A tiny droplet fell from the cloud,
filled with gifts spiritually endowed.
It descended amidst God's radiance
to seek its earthly residence.

A minute spot of moisture round,
Settled upon the warm soft ground.
Nature's depth of welcoming
Filled it through to envelop him.

The droplet's heart was filled with glee,
For he thought what he would like to be.
Desire struck with a mighty blow
About the gifts that he must know.

Traveling down into the earth,
Telling his wealth within his girth.
To share it with true ecstasy,
Among the creatures he would see.

Soon he heard a thundering roar,
That shook where he stood on the soily floor.
The creatures scattered as fast as they could,
But he didn't move. He stayed where he stood.

The earth heaved and rolled
and spun him around,
The next thing he knew
His spot was unsound.

The earth opened up and down he fell,
Into a steaming, watery well.
He floated around in this dungeon place,
Wondering if this was his resting place.

He looked around and to his surprise,
Droplets like him had the same surmise.
They clung together as they swirled and twirled,
Not knowing where they would next be hurled.

Confusion and tension lurked at their side,
Bringing fear-ridden feelings in a drive to do right.
It came abrupt, their violent encounter,
Walls filled a space and rotted asunder.

All droplets dispersed hither and yon,
Into unknown cracks and fissures beyond.
A droplet fell through a darkened abyss,
Hitting out jutted rocks, he just couldn't miss.

43

He tried to touch the slippery wall,
There was nothing to grasp to break his fall.

Terrified thoughts raced through his mind.
Was he to live in a place of this kind?
Tumbling, falling, not knowing where,
Or did the Creator not really care?

When suddenly from way down below,
A shimmering ray began to glow.
Its radiance burst to a brilliant light
In a rainbow of colors; what a glorious sight.

He splashed upon a rocky place,
Where God caressed him in a spiritual embrace.
His terrified thoughts no longer could live,
For God had filled him with his love to give.

He nestled into a shiny stone,
Immediately, he knew this was his home.
Pressed deeply into the soul of Mother Earth,
He would be nurtured to await his rebirth.

God's radiance of love was felt and seen,
For the rocks were sharing his essence supreme.
If only we could glow and shine like them.
"You can," saith God, at a birth of a gem.

3

on communing with nature, attaining self-attunement, and going into the silence

From the teachings of Twylah:

"It is time to commune with nature." These were the words that opened the way for Seneca Indian instruction. The teacher was Moses Shongo, the last of the Seneca Medicine doctors. I can see him now sitting on the porch of our home on the Cattaraugus Indian Reservation. I sat on one of the stone slabs which served as steps leading to the entrance of our home.

The white rambling farmhouse was my birthplace. It was built by my great-grandfather in 1858 after the Senecas lost their beloved Buffalo Reservation. The house stood like the hub of a wheel with the majestic sugar maples nodding in the gentle breeze.

Our home was designed so that the forces of nature streamed through from the east to west, from the back door to the front, as the Sun traveled the skypath. My grandfather's chair occupied the north corner of the porch. It wrapped around his bulky form, as he snuggled down upon its squeaky springs. When he was deep in thought, his fingers tapped rhythmically on the armrest.

I watched him in profound wonderment and followed him in action every day. My eyes were drawn to the tanned fedora hat that had acquired a personality all its own. A crop of jet-black hair, shiny as a raven, peaked beneath the brim of his hat. His sparkling eyes were pools of wisdom, transmitting his innate love. While his face beamed with a smile, it radiated spiritual brotherhood. He could be likened to a big tree, the greatest compliment of our ancestors. He stood proud and erect, looking deep into the essence of Mother Earth, always affirming thanksgiving for her gifts.

At the close of each day, facing the west, he watched the Sun, the center of our universe, slowly descend beyond the trees. "Prepare yourself for the lessons of the Great Spirit," Grandfather would say. My eyes beheld the burning aura, silently sinking to the rim of the sky. A glorious sensation prepared me for the sanctity of the Sky Dome, the place of spiritual tranquility. An ebon essence brushed across my face, as I was borne aloft.

The Golden Dome, abounding in iridescent splendor, filled my senses with vitalizing awareness. Then, a whisper, steeped in solemnity, echoed within me. It was the voice of the Great Spirit.

I had prepared myself well, as I had been taught, and I was ready for whatever Grandfather was inspired to tell me. I can hear his strong voice now, speaking to me of the ways of our people.

In his learned way, as his ancestors taught, he would say, "Long before there was time, place, or even human beings, there was a Great Spirit." I cannot recall a time when this statement did not preface the lessons I was to hear. It rings in my mind to this day, filling me with the peace and reverence that only spiritual feeling can express.

Many long years ago, our ancestors trod paths along the animal trails that had been made before them. These passageways carved the shortest and safest distances between neighboring villages and distant nations, where Indians traveled to exchange cultural views, customs, and traditions.

The wisdom of life is learned from the greatest teacher, Mother Earth.

Countless examples of nature's perfection, splendor, and harmony are manifested all around the early Indians. A central wisdom, known by all Medicine doctors as a secret of the ages, asserts that self-understanding is a *desire*; that self-discipline is a *key*; self-control, a *way*; self-realization, the *goal*. The word that encompassed the secret is *communication*. There is a belief that everyone in every nation still acts as a guardian over this secret.

I recall that one of the greatest lessons my grandfather ever taught me was a discussion of the principles that were followed to promote personal happiness among the early Seneca. "How well do you communicate?" was the question he asked, in his soft, even-modulated voice. "Communicating is understanding. Understanding leads toward peace of mind. Peace of mind leads toward happiness. Happiness is communicating."

These four statements constitute the symbolism of the circle, which embodies spiritual harmony. If problems should arise in your life, the blame can be placed on a lack of communication. We communicate in various ways with every breath we take. Personal happiness should stem from principles developed through routines of daily living regarding the ways we communicate.

A breakdown in personal communication, in many cases, will cause four reactions: 1. Anger; 2. Withdrawal from the person or the situation that influenced the breakdown; 3. Flight, running away from the person or situation identified with the breakdown; 4. The creation of excuses for not facing the situation in order to solve it.

These reactions fall under the heading of immaturity. Immaturity is the basic reason for failure in life, school, work, family, or marriage. No one wants to admit to being immature, yet our reactions may reflect such a condition in spite of ourselves.

The following are two thoughts of wisdom:

We cannot reap happiness while wallowing in the mire of immaturity, because immaturity fosters emotional chaos, self-degradation, and depravity.

Immaturity permits thoughts of guilt to be nurtured with seeds of peace and love.

The question is, what can we do about immaturity? The first step is to recognize that a problem exists. If a breach occurs in your life-style, there is a problem. A breach is any rupture that causes a situation, a separation, insecurity, or disharmony.

Carefully study the four reactions. Can you identify them as belonging to you? If you can, the first step has been faced. At this point, you have recognized that an inner force is available to help you reinforce your desire for making an honest self-analysis. You have tapped into your creative mind, your place of highest gift. Everyone possesses this gift and the ability to use it—that is, if the individual has the desire to solve the problem.

The longer a problem is allowed to exist, the harder it is to return to peace of mind. When a problem exists, you tend to bring others to the dilemma. It takes self-discipline to face and to accept the blame for causing a problem to exist. Our thoughts and actions account for our living in a state of conflict. Such a state results in mental restlessness and often illness. Our thoughts can drain our physical energy.

Set the controls with self-discipline and by sharing the best of yourself with others, travel the road with peace of mind. In order to measure your ability to communicate, self-awareness must be sharpened. You do this by tapping into your highest intellectual or creative mind. Then, you understand how to enjoy peace of mind, general good health, and gain self-satisfaction—not only within yourself, but within others who are in your environment.

The second step is to adapt yourself to faith. We are not born in faith. It is a characteristic that must be developed. Faith needs to dwell within as a part of our nature before we can sincerely enjoy sharing it with others. It is the sharing that brings the most happiness and the feeling of well-being.

Parents play a vital role in developing faith patterns in their children. Because some parents do not inject faithful characteristics in their daily lives, they tend to tear down, rather than build, faith in their children. We learn through example. For this reason, take time to evaluate the home environment that helps establish your way of life.

You may recognize extending a bad state of affairs into your life from the unthinking examples affecting your personal development. To accept this unthinking shows a lack of maturity.

Successful communication depends on self-understanding and a reasonable amount of faith. Only when personal faith patterns have been developed can we find what pressures and tensions have the ability to devour a secure image.

When a dimension of faith is lost, we withdraw into a shell of self-pity, caring for nothing, not even for ourselves. We live out our lives in personal thought patterns that serve as habits and behavior traits. When these thought patterns fall into undesirable habits, they rob us of peace of mind and health; and they often bring on creative confusion that affects those who happen to be under our influence. Measuring our abilities to communicate self-awareness must be sharpened. I emphasize this because it is so important.

Free yourself from negative influence. Negative thoughts are the old habits that gnaw at the roots of the soul. When these negative habits flare up, counteract them by flooding your mind with a powerful thought, one that disciplines your personality. It is incredible how this technique has the power to reinforce the positive action. The more this technique is practiced, the easier the negative thought is erased. A surge of new confidence and strength will stream through your body, as this achievement takes hold.

Self-realization is the goal. Put this affirmation at the tip of your tongue. Nurture these words of wisdom and make them part of your life-style. Such an affirmation is the umbilical cord of creativity. You are born with the ability to attain self-realization. There is no reason for your failure in life-style, because by this lesson you have been enlightened to see that wisdom is yours to use.

This brought to an end one of the greatest lessons my grandfather ever taught. If it had not been for this lesson and the wisdom of my people, I would have been crushed beneath the vibrations of immature people I have met and smothered with my own self-indulgent rituals of immaturity. I am sharing this wisdom and spiritual insight with you, feeling secure that the infinite Great Spirit guides you and tells you what to do.

Before any human beings, there was the Great Spirit.

After preparing the Sun and Moon and Water and setting them into place, the Great Spirit made patterns for all things which were to be born and arranged for all happenings which were to occur. Then the Great Spirit prepared Nature Land where all things were to mingle in harmony. Next the Great Spirit caused creatures to be evolved, from plants to creatures that swam, crawled, walked, and flew. As they evolved, gifts were bestowed upon them, with abilities to learn lessons from one another.

All things are sent and belong to the Great Spirit. For this reason, the Spirit is in everything that breathes, senses, hears, tastes, smells, sees. The Spirit is in all emotions, and it is present at birth and at death. The inhabitants of Nature Land are aware of the Great Spirit through the whisperings that speak through the mind.

It is time to commune with Nature; Her knowledge of life we drink.
She lays her wealth before us, and hopes that we'll learn to think.

We're filled with events for learning;
When comforts brought ease, it dimmed our yearning.

In the very beginning, the Seneca were drawn close to nature. Legends related the wonders of nature and its effect on all creatures and plants. It was not long before the ancestors of the Senecas sensed a powerful force revealed all around them. Some were able to feel the force; others were able to see it. They called the force *Swen-i-o*, the Great Mystery.

The lessons nature taught set a pattern for Senecas to follow. They soon learned that each Indian must find a way to fit into this pattern in order to experience a sense of happiness. By the process of trial and error, a series of techniques evolved that helped the people develop a thorough and more meaningful use of their minds.

In the atmosphere of the forest, they recognized the presence of the Great Mystery. Its force penetrated into every soul, making every soul a part of it. This was where nature influenced the life of the early Senecas. This rhythm blended all creatures into complete harmony, instilling the habitual silence of the Seneca as a characteristic.

When alone with his thoughts, he listened and *heard* the Silence.

He listened and *saw* the Silence.

He listened and *tasted* the Silence.

He closed his eyes and *felt* the Silence deep within.

The woodlands became his chapel; his body, the altar.

In the Silence, he began to communicate with his Creator, and he received peace.

In solitude, he felt his thoughts being guided to a higher intellectual level. The feeling of belonging to nature brought him back, time and time again, to be enchanted by the Great Mystery.

It was only natural that the early people sought these quiet moments, for it was their first realization of spiritual love. Nature was Mother Earth, the caretaker of all creatures and plants. They needed to share her gifts with others in faith, work, love, and pleasure.

Learning the unspoken language of the inhabitants who live in the forest helped the Seneca to understand the necessity for having a purpose in life—to live in harmony with self and with nature. The Senecas accepted the kinship of all creatures and plants of nature. The Senecas believed all creatures and plants were equal in the eyes of nature, each performing its specific talents according to its abilities.

Whenever the Seneca fell out of balance with nature, they caused conditions of discord. Discord caused the illnesses, frustrations, and disasters that visited them. When the Seneca developed spiritual equality and a life of spiritual balance, they became a mature people of wisdom.

The Senecas taught their children the importance of identifying themselves with all creatures and plants of nature. This was the first step in helping the children to see the problems that all creatures and plants must overcome in order to stay in harmony with nature. They learned the difference between the creatures, but they felt the same spirit flowing throughout all of them.

Feeling to the Seneca can be described as his faith. The depth of his feeling was measured by the depth of his faith. Learning how to identify this depth depended upon the ability to recognize the different levels of feeling through self-knowledge.

The early Seneca recognized that there was a spiritual feeling and a material feeling. Spiritual feeling can be unlimited, whereas material feeling has its limitations. In the spiritual level dwelt all desires. Material feelings were a result of material experiences relying upon the senses—seeing, hearing, smelling, and tasting.

One of the methods used to understand spiritual feelings as compared with material feelings is as follows:

Close your eyes and look straight ahead. Look out behind the eyelids. These are the spiritual eyes. What you see depends upon your personal experiences. Open your eyes, and these are the material eyes. Many times they fool you.

The second step is to listen for your heartbeat. Become aware of the feelings you experience while listening to your heartbeat. This is going within. This is when you realize that maybe your heartbeat is becoming a little *less* pronounced. And then you establish a balance within yourself. This balance is the point of relaxation where you feel comfortable. Everyone can find this.

Open your eyes, and make a self-evaluation of what you've accomplished.

Faith was the first stepping stone that led toward love, work, and eventually pleasure. Faith gave a strong feeling of belonging to something, or someone. In the beginning, the something was Mother Earth. All Indians had faith in Mother Earth.

A small child nestled in its mother's protective arms feels the first level of faith. As faith grows, the depth of feeling becomes evident. The physical contact of mother and child causes faith to flow between them, as feeling. Therefore, feeling needs to be present to express the first stages of faith.

The habit of being faithful was considered on a spiritual level. All forms of creativity were believed to be gifts of the Creator. If these habits had their roots in the spiritual level, creativeness and actions were more easily controlled—and were better understood.

Because faith had become established and feeling was present, adding the ingredient of warmth led to love. Where there was no feeling, there was no faith; so faith and feeling appeared to go hand in hand. To the Seneca Indian, extending the open hand became a symbol of faith. The degree of faith began to manifest itself by different degrees of warmth.

To the early Seneca, love was a feeling that had grown from the seed of faith. The degree of love was measured by the feeling of warmth. The Sun was revered by the Indians because of its love for the nature people. It shared its warmth with them. Through self-discipline the Indian had to control the amount of love he accepted from nature, as well as that which he was willing and able to share with others. You have to know how much warmth you can accept—or you will be burned to a crisp.

Love, faith, and work cannot be measured without feeling.

The level of hearing, seeing, smelling, and tasting cannot be measured without a degree of feeling. Faith, nourished with deep feeling, developed the warmth of love. Continued faithful actions on the part of an individual toward others created good feelings. Its warmth could be felt when people assembled.

The feeling of warmth appeared more intense between a mother and her child. It was always present where families gathered. Faith and warm love lived together. Where one was, you could always find the other. The Sun, therefore, was a symbol of love to the early Senecas. It soothed his soul.

The circle, the shape of the Sun, took on an added significance; it was symbolic of perfection and equality. The Sun's color was the most revered because of its beauty and magnificence. The Indians found themselves smiling whenever the Sun shone upon them. They believed that the Sun smiled at them all the time.

Smiling at someone and placing one's hand in another's signified the presence of love. To smile at someone was to convey a spiritual message of good will. Words were not always necessary where faith and love were present. The feelings that accompany love speak for themselves.

The Senecas held a fixed purpose in life, and that was to learn about the Great Mystery. To them, the Great Spirit was the Great Mystery.

The Great Spirit—the Divine Supreme, Maker of All Things, Now and Forever.

The Great Spirit—the Eternal Mind, whose thoughts flow everlastingly.

The Great Spirit—the Master Designer, the Arranger of Patterns of All and Everything.

The Great Spirit—the Celestial Law, the Perpetuator of Perfection.

The Great Spirit—the Ethereal Voice, the Composer of the Harmony in Nature.

The Great Spirit—the Great Mystery, God.

Going into the Silence meant communing with nature in spirit, mind and body. Nature's atmosphere radiated the spirituality of the Supreme Power and provided the path that led the early Seneca into the Great Silence.

The legend of the First Messenger of Swen-i-o, the Great Mystery, tells of the encounter with the spiritual essence that was responsible for the practice of going into the Silence.

Four very old people, two men and two women who were endowed with great wisdom gleaned throughout their advancing years, sat in the woodlands on the warm earth near a brooklet that crept beneath a canopy of leaves and branches. They had come to reminisce of their kindred experiences when suddenly the heavens opened:

A Glorious Beam of Light
In All Its Brilliant Splendor
Gently Drifted Over Them
Seeding Peace and Solemnity
On Everything It Touched.

They watched in wonderment, spellbound by the Light's sublime magnificence. It filtered through their bodies, cleansing them of all infirmities.

Presently, they were borne aloft to a place of divine ecstasy, where the "Secret of the Ages" was revealed to them, telling of things to be. They saw the first messenger of the Supreme Power: the spiritual hand with outstretched fingers and thumb. The message was *"Ens-wy-stawg,"* meaning, "It comes through." This was the first spiritual experience of "going into Silence."

The symbolism of the hand signifies that as the thumb assists the four fingers in life, unity, equality, and eternity, so does the Supreme Power or Great Spirit assist all things in nature.

From that time on, the four people of wisdom spent their remaining days communing with nature in reverence and solitude. Their spiritual insight increased as others joined them to listen to their words of wisdom and spiritual counseling.

From this revelation the entire custom of sitting in council evolved. It became evident that the messengers of the Great Spirit wore many faces. They could be manifestations of nature, creatures, or earthly forces.

The Secret of the Ages revolved around attitudes and thoughts that instilled a sense of brotherhood with all creation. Its practice was carried on as a personal attribute in solitude with one's own thoughts in direct communication with the Creator. It mattered not when or where it was held, since the body was the chapel that housed the spiritual light.

The following procedure was found to be helpful in entering the Silence:

The Indian discovered that wherever he went he could find a stone. After selecting one of his choice, the stone was placed in the palm of the left hand with the right hand clasped on top. Holding the stone in this fashion created a union of forces within the hand. When this pulsating was felt, the Indian believed he had raised himself into the vibrational current of a higher spiritual level. The stone acted as a reminder that everything was of the same source—the spiritual brotherhood of all and everything.

The following mental procedure was also useful in entering the Silence. It helped the Indian locate a place in his mind where peace and contentment lived.

You are walking into the woods. Your feet are plotting a path on the soft, spongy ground. The path is narrow and winds around trees and bushes so that, at times, you need to duck under the low-hanging branches.

Through the clearing ahead lies a shimmering lake. The Sun spreads a rainbow of colors across the rippling surface.

Upon reaching the water's edge, you stand quietly and listen to the lapping surf, as it pushes the pebbles back and forth on the clean, warm sand. To the left is a log inviting you to sit upon its blanket of moss. You accept the invitation and settle down upon the cushioned softness, feeling it press against your body.

A breeze carrying the woodland aromas brushes your hair and caresses your face. The trees are singing the songs of nature in harmony.

The Silence majestically weaves its magic spell, as it gathers all nature within its fold. At last, the serenity of spiritual Silence flows into your every fiber, drenching it with divine purity.

You listen and *hear* the Silence.
You listen and *see* the Silence.
You listen and *smell* the Silence.

You listen and *taste* the Silence.
You listen and *feel* the embrace of the Silence.

Peering through the spiritual eyes, you find the real you
dwelling therein. While drifting along with the ebbing tide
of spirituality, you and Nature become one, together plucking
these tender moments of intimate reunion with the Supreme
Power, the Great Spirit.

The Great Spirit, Divine Supreme
Maker of all and everything.
The Great Spirit, the Eternal Mind
Whose thoughts flow everlastingly.
The Great Spirit, the Master Designer
Arranger of patterns of all and everything.

Faith in oneself makes work an enjoyment; adventures in
knowledge lead toward attunement.

Nature's caretaker is Mother Earth
Her gifts of provision begin at each birth.
We learn from our forebears the secret of use
Obeying these guidelines prevents self-abuse.

4

the symbolism of four

Why is the number four sacred to the Amerindian?

TWYLAH: Remember when the four ancient ones ascended in the Light to the Great Mystery and saw the extended hand?

They learned that the symbolism of four was present in this extended hand; it meant life, unity, equality, and eternity. It also meant seeing, smelling, tasting, and hearing. These four senses could not function without feeling. Feeling includes touch and all emotion. When the hand is clasped, it is the symbol of unity. Unity is the spiritual law that binds the entire universe.

They descended with a feeling of being completely healed of all the thoughts they had that were not right. From this experience they saw how the Pathway of Peace should be followed and how the great lessons should be learned. They learned at this time that self-knowledge was the key; self-understanding was the desire; self-control was the way, and self-realization was the goal.

They discovered that everything goes in a circle, and that communication is the key to the pathway of learning. They learned communication means understanding; understanding means peace of mind; peace of mind leads toward happiness; therefore, happiness is communicating. A circle again!

And consider these symbolic representations of the number four:

The first four Creations were Sun, Moon, Water, Earth.

The four laws of Creation are life, unity, equality, eternity.

The four seasons are spring, summer, fall, winter.

The four directions are east, north, west, south.

The four races of Creation are white, red, yellow, black.

The four senses of feeling are seeing, hearing, tasting, smelling.

The four guidelines toward self-development are the following:

Am I happy doing what I am doing?

What am I doing to add to the confusion?

What am I doing to bring about peace and contentment?

How will I be remembered when I am gone—in absence and in death?

The four requirements of good health are food, sleep, cleanliness, good thoughts.

The four divisions of nature are spirit, mind, body, life.

The four divisions of goals are faith, love, work, pleasure.

The four ages of development are the learning age, the age of adoption, the age of improvement, the age of wisdom.

The four expressions of sharing are making others feel

you care; an expression of interest (everything in creation has something to offer; listen and learn); an expression of friendship (promotes spiritual growth); an expression of belonging (sharing of goals toward a higher spiritual growth).

My grandfather, Moses Shongo, spent so much time breaking things down in fours. He taught me to do things in fours, and all my life I have done this. When I iron clothes, I iron in fours. I iron four things and put them away. Then four more. When I clean, I clean in fours. If I don't do things this way, I don't feel good. If I don't satisfy myself in doing something, I don't bother doing it. It is amazing how it works.

Unity is the great spiritual law, and we can break that down into four parts, as well:

1. Unity is going into the Silence in spirit, mind, and body.

2. It is a union through which all spirituality flows.

3. It is a goal toward communicating with all things in nature.

4. It is recognized by the intellect through the senses, through the emotions, and through impressions.

Unity is the law of nature. I have known this since I can remember. Everything has its place, and everything works in unison. If you get in trouble, it is because you have created some static in this unified picture. You have only yourself to deal with. You only have control over yourself; therefore, you have to begin there. Equality to the Indian meant that everything in this universe had a place.

5

guiding youth
amerindian style

TWYLAH: An old Indian adage says, "If you do not like what your children are doing, stop what you are doing."

The Indians never tried to push any ideas on anyone else, not even within their own families. The responsibility of the parents was to guide the child, and they recognized that the child was not going to follow the path of either the father or the mother. The child would be developing his own life-style.

That's very difficult for many parents to accept.

If I say to one of the people, "Would you like to have your youngster join the dancing group?" the mother will answer, "Oh, I'd love to have him join, but I have to ask him." The decision is up to the individual. Therefore, if somebody is doing something that everybody else thinks is wrong, no one will interfere, because as long as that person is happy doing what he is doing, nobody will try to change it.

Neither, of course, should we imply that the Indian child always gets his way. Last night when Louis asked to stay overnight with a friend, there was no hesitation on his grandmother's part to deny him the request.

Oh, no. But you see, Louis called; he wouldn't just go ahead and do it.

And there was no whining. He asked over the telephone, "Can I talk to Grandma?" I said, "We're busy now; may I help you?" He said, "I just got home, Twylah, and I'd like to stay overnight with my friend." I said, "Well, I'll ask her." He told me, "I'm sorry I'm disturbing you." I asked, and Grandma said no. I told him, "You're out of luck, Louis." And he said, "Okay, fine." That's all there was to it.

Certainly he was disappointed, but he didn't go into a tizzy about it and make a big noise so finally Grandma would say yes. But you see, you can't have a double standard. And this is one thing that the Indian did not have. There was none of the philosophy that dictated that when you become a parent you can do things you couldn't do as a child.

All over the Indian nations, the one thing that stood out was that, if you said you were going to do something, you did it. Your word was your bond, and if you made a promise, you kept it. And if you could not, you didn't say that you would.

Years ago, if a person broke his word, it was considered a gross crime. If a person did an injustice to someone else, the crime was brought before everyone; and the person would be tried, so to speak, before the council. If someone stole something, all of his possessions were taken from him except what he had on his back, and all his possessions were destroyed in front of everyone. The shame that went with this made one think before he would transgress against a tribesman. This was why the Indians never had to lock up their homes. Everyone had respect for the possessions of everyone else.

Did I ever explain the origin of the term "Indian giver"?

All right, I gave Marilyn that necklace, because I wanted her to have it. She didn't have one, so I gave this necklace to her. If I came out to Iowa, and I saw her several times—I don't say that she has to wear it all the time—but if she never wore it and just put it in a drawer, and she wasn't using it, and if I had another friend who would like to have a necklace, I would say to Marilyn, "You're not using the necklace, are you?" And I would expect her to say no. Then she would say, "It isn't that I don't like the necklace, but I don't have the occasion to use it." She would give it back to me, and then I would give it to someone who would use it.

That is where the expression "Indian giver" originated. But it does not mean to give, then to take away. It means to reclaim an unused gift and give it to someone who has need of it. Years ago the Indians did the things that they could do the best. Each person selected the thing he could do the best and enjoy the most. In turn, he would share the fruits of his labor with someone else. Therefore, if someone needed blankets, we would go to the woman who made blankets. If she needed something that we could provide, she would come to us. It was almost like a barter system.

But if a weaver found someone not using the blanket that he had been given, the weaver would take it away and give it to someone who needed it. A fruit of labor was made to be used, not made to be saved. This was the principle. That is where the "Indian giver" thing comes out. There are many things that are told only partway.

The Indian puts no monetary value on the gifts. The Sun and Moon gave their light; the Mother Earth nurtured plants; the rain and air gave to everyone. This was their work. The Indians gave the things they knew and loved the best.

The best hunters and arrow-makers taught their trade. The value of the work was in the use and in the happiness given the user. The reward for making others happy was a service that had been rendered.

Work was doing for others. Play was a method of instruction and a means of self-development. Joining in games was a means of self-discipline and self-control. It was more important to the Seneca to develop his talents and abilities than to win. Dexterity outweighed strength. Learning skills and developing endurance were the goals. Contests were based on acquiring skill. Play, therefore, was a method of developing ability. His environment was careless, so play was a pleasant way for the Indian to master the skills necessary to live with safety and to build personal faith and self-confidence.

Pleasure was the feeling of happiness gained through achieving success, for the players and for the enjoyment by the spectators. Those happy feelings were shared, because both gave part of themselves. The players displayed their skill and ability. The spectators gave their attention and enjoyment.

It is very important that discipline be on a spiritual level. If parents live and instruct from this level, they raise the emotional level of their children. Punishment of the physical body does not have the same results, because the parents should be seeking to develop the spiritual mind, and when they punish the physical body, they have created only a momentary hurt. Instead of encouraging spiritual uplift-ment, a physical hurt encourages anger.

This happened at Christmastime last year. Janice was here with the two boys. They had a little toy that we had given them, and they were playing with it. Michael was four and the little one was a toddler.

Janice, Diane, and I went in the kitchen, and the rest of the family were in the living room. The boys were running around and around.

Joe, Janice's husband, said, "Michael, stop your running!" Janice came from the kitchen and said, "Michael, if you would stop your running, Dee wouldn't chase you. Besides, you or Dee might get hurt on that terrazzo floor."

"No, Mom," Dee said; so they continued to run.

The boys had been told that they were not to be doing this. But they were obviously happy in what they were doing, because the little boy said no, he wouldn't get hurt.

After a couple of more times around, Dee fell and stubbed his toes. I came into the picture.

Michael is the older and the example to the younger. His father had told him to stop running as an order, and at that moment a certain degree of anger had come over him and had motivated him to run all the more.

"Michael," I said, "are you happy doing what you are doing?" He looked at the little fellow crying on the floor. "No, Grandma." He used his intellectuality and learned a lesson.

Michael went over and picked up his brother and said, "I am sorry, Dee." He was big enough to take the blame. He learned.

Who was responsible? The child was responsible for the action, and he knew in this case that he was responsible. The younger one will always do what the older one does. They are little apes; they want to follow in the footsteps of their older brothers and sisters. And both the younger and older children want to be like the parents. Therefore, the parents have to set an example for their children.

Living is a chain reaction: Everyone looks to one who has had the experience before him, so that he can try the experience on for size. If it fits well, he will use it.

Later on that same day, the boys were talking back and forth about a toy. "It's my turn!" "No, it's my turn!" "Mom, he's not sharing!"

Dee came to report how Michael had taken the toy.

Grandma came into the picture again. I asked, "Are you happy now that you have the toy?" "Yes," Michael said. He really wasn't, however. He momentarily was, but he had taken it from his brother.

I said, "You don't want to play with your brother, do you? Go with your happiness and the toy to the utility room, and you stay there until you are no longer happy."

He was out there for some time, but pretty soon it was, "Grandma, Dee can have the toy now. I have run out of my happiness."

Michael gave up the toy, and he handed it to Dee. Dee said, "I want to go back there and be happy, too!" So he went back to the utility room with his happiness and his toy and he played. The boys learned something, and there was no swatting.

My son-in-law looked at me and said, "You have the patience of a saint!"

No, I was thinking. And I was trying to teach what I knew to these kids. I had been taught to think. This is what education should be—to teach people how to think. You can't do this unless you know yourself. It takes self-discipline and self-control. These are the two basic things.

6

a class session
in a seneca longhouse

There were, perhaps, twenty of us. Neither Marilyn nor I were concerned about such mundane journalistic minutiae as how many people were in attendance or what they wore or how they looked. They were our brothers and sisters. We were gathered in the original Seneca longhouse from the old Buffalo Creek Reservation. Our teacher was a woman wise in the traditional ways of her people, a woman totally imbued with Seneca Wisdom.

Earlier that day, Twylah had shared with us her private Medicine place. We had walked with her in the autumn-like warmth of an early December day and followed her through the woods until we had come to a place on the side of a hill where a spring bubbled and flowed toward a grassy meadow. This was Twylah's favorite place for going into the Silence.

This was where she replenished her spirit and received insights from the Great Mystery.

Now she stood before us as an instructor, gently authoritative, smilingly firm. There was no question who was in charge.

Twylah pushed the "play" button of a cassette recorder and released the haunting music that had come to her in a vision from the Great Mystery. A friend had played the piece on an organ after transcribing it from Twylah's humming and singing; and now the captured tones guided us through the first phase of our class session in a Seneca longhouse.

"Walk to the music," Twylah told us. "Drop off at a chair that is in a place that feels comfortable to you. In order to do what we're going to do tonight, we want everyone to feel very, very comfortable."

As we walked about the longhouse, one did not need to be a psychometrist (one who feels and interprets psychically the history of an inanimate object) to sense the vibrations of the invisible tribesmen of the great Iroquois nation who moved their feet in cadence with our own. Grandfathers and grandmothers who had long since—in Earth time—passed to the Spirit World returned to their old longhouse that night to join us in a sharing of Seneca Wisdom.

After everyone had selected his place, Twylah began:

"I explained to you last week about the seven stones, and that the seven stones are radiating color. As we step on these stones, we will be able to feel the color, and perhaps see it. We will work on this with four senses: the sense of hearing, the sense of tasting, the sense of smelling, and the sense of seeing.

"In some of the classes that I have been conducting, we

have experimented to find which way is the most success-ful for each of us. So we're going to do this tonight, to re-affirm which procedure will be the best for each individual. Some of you, I know, have had experience in seeing. I know some of you know exactly what you are going to do. But there are others who have not experienced those things, espe-cially the young people here. And I'm delighted to have them here, because the young people have not developed so many inhibitions as the oldsters have. For this reason, they will perhaps remember this experience tonight all their lives. So we will start.

"Feel the spiritual light flow into your feet. You can feel your body begin to fill up as a vessel, as spiritual light flows up through your legs. Now I'm not going to tell you how fast it flows, because this is what you will be doing. I'm simply telling you it flows up your body, up to the top of your head.

"From this point your entire body is completely filled with the spiritual light, and it begins to radiate out as far as you want it to, which is usually the distance of your arms out-stretched at the top of your head, and you describe a circle within this area. But please do not limit it. This is a rekin-dling of the spiritual light, and it makes you aware of the spiritual essence that is constantly present within your physi-cal body.

"After you have done this, think of the sounds that you hear. Then think of the taste that you are aware of. So it's what you hear first, then what you taste, and after that, what you smell. Last, what you can see.

"And when you look, keep your eyes closed and look out the back of your eyelids. These are your spiritual eyes, and what you see is unlimited.

73

"After you have gone through these four stages, decide which is the best procedure for you to become completely relaxed and to feel yourself begin to walk on the Pathway of Peace.

"We will do this in silence for a while, and then I will explain the Pathway of Peace.

"This is what you need to do in order to feel the creative essence flowing within your physical body. We will now stand at the threshold of the Pathway of Peace.

"There are seven stones. Each stone will have a certain radiance. As you step upon the first stone, which has seven sides, you will stand there, and you will request the assistance of a messenger of the Creator—or if you like, a spiritual hand. You never walk alone. The spiritual hand is always there to assist you.

"You step upon the first stone, and a color will come to you. You remain there until you feel you are ready to step onto the second stone. Each time you step on a stone, another color will manifest itself.

"As you step from one stone to another, you will eventually reach the seventh stone. This stone will be radiating a color similar to violet. You are at the doorway of entering the Silence.

"You may be able to walk the path very fast; but let the impressions come through just exactly the way you feel. When you reach the seventh step, you have opened yourself up to the flow of the Infinite Spirit, and you are then ready for any revelation or gift to be presented to you.

"Each one will do as he feels in going into the Silence.

"We will now sit in complete silence. Try to proceed the best way you can.

"When you have reached the point you wish, come back the way that suits you best. When you again reach the bottom, or the first stone, and you step back into the material world, say a prayer of thanksgiving for this wonderful experience.

"In ancient times, when students wanted to follow a path, they would go to a teacher. He or she would suggest to them the same as I have to you. I would have you find your own way to walk on the stones. Each one of you have a way.

"Don't let color disturb you. This may be all you get. It is good.

"There isn't anything that is bad.

"I can't emphasize this enough. Every experience is emotional. When you feel it emotionally, you have been taught a lesson.

"In spite of the fact that you may say you are not doing it well, you are learning."

Each person went into the Silence, employing Twylah's meditative technique of visualizing the seven stepping stones to the Spirit. After several minutes had passed, Twylah recalled us to the reality we shared on the Earth plane. She asked each person to tell what feeling he had employed —hearing, smelling, tasting, seeing—and to describe the colors in which the stones had appeared to him. Upon the completion of each recitation, Twylah would interpret the meaning of the colors and the things seen, heard, smelled, or tasted by the student.

TWYLAH: Now we are going to do something entirely different. I am going to play the music; and as you listen, let yourself go. I am not going to talk. There will be another experience. I hope this will help you understand yourself better.

Twylah punched the cassette and the strains of her song once more filled the longhouse with most remarkable vibrations. After playing the tape through and permitting us to sit for several minutes in silence, Twylah called for us to present our responses and experiences. Again she offered interpretations of the symbols received on the musical "trip."

TWYLAH: One time in class, I used these words to help suggest feeling: As you walk on the soft ground, you can feel the leaves beneath you. You have to duck as you walk beneath the low branches. You look ahead and you see a lake, and you see the Sun with different reflections on the lake. You sit on a log. Feel the soft moss pressing against your body. Smell the aroma that is around you. You get your various senses going, and then you feel yourself floating up and up. You see the real you.

At the end I asked the people to open their eyes. They all sat there. I waited a little bit and asked them again. No one responded. I waited a little longer, and I wondered what was going on. Finally a girl in the corner said, "Why don't you shut up! I have never had such a wonderful experience."

Another time when I used this music, a young man in the class began to cry. I asked him what the problem was. He said it made him feel sad. I said, "It certainly isn't sad music to my ears." He said, "It is life. It is life in my ears."

These are different experiences of the music for different people. There are different moods of the music throughout.

I think this music was given to me through my grandfather. He was a wonderful musician. He taught music at Albuquerque.

In order to make going into the Silence easier to accomplish, I suggest the "four P's": Purpose, Preparation, Procedure, and Progression.

The purpose of going into the Silence is to establish a personal routine that will become a regular experience for spiritual enrichment in your life-style. Everyone is searching for personal enrichment. How one goes about it depends on the individual.

The preparation is so important for this solitary meditation that it should be done as carefully as we prepare our food. Spiritual nourishment is the result, and it is really not only the lifeline, but a guideline for our very existence. It seems the more we become aware of our potential, the more we have the opportunity to enjoy peace. Of course, the best procedure is whichever way you can determine that best helps you to obtain this feeling of ecstasy.

To the Seneca, going into the Silence means a cleansing of feelings which are brought in by his environment.

During this time, the physical body goes through a state of being cleansed and renewed. This is the important thing. Not only to be cleansed, but to be renewed.

We must resist those thoughts and actions which limit spiritual cleansing. We constantly are resisting things without even thinking.

The disciplined person entertains feelings that contribute toward his happiness. Feelings are believed responsible for actions in Seneca life and are considered the real motivations behind one's desire. It is necessary to maintain a physical balance between nature and oneself, in order to receive spiritual cleansing in spirit, mind, and body. Balance between self and nature is an individual feeling where one feels satisfaction. This is where you have to find that you are satisfied.

This seeking of balance is constantly affecting you, and your emotions are going up and down. As a result, the physical body is trying to adjust to these emotions. After a while your physical body is drained and you don't know why.

That brings up something else—streams of energy. The moment you recognize that your energy has been drained, you have raised yourself to a high spiritual level where you can do something about it. If you have never been introduced to the fact that people and things can drain your energy, you can go along and wonder what is the matter with you. You are tired; you become irritable; then your body suffers, because its functioning level has been lowered. Now what do you do? The moment you see or feel that your energy has been drained, look around and see what did it. If there are people around, look about and see who did it. Nine times out of ten, the person who drained your energy is uplifted.

You will find in an office situation that there are usually two people who drain everyone else's energy. This is my observation. When the two people come to work, they are tired. After they have been on the job awhile, they begin to perk up. They are gnawing away, sniping; but they are becoming energized.

You can do something about it. The moment you feel the draining of energy, counteract it by sending a very powerful good thought to them. If they turn around and call you a dirty name, you turn around and send them a good thought.

I have developed this technique, and it really works: When someone is agitated and they are uptight and things are really bad, *I mentally put them into a drain tile!* The drain tile completely covers them, and I can't see their heads. It is open at the top and at the bottom. The drain tile, in my mind, opens them up to the spiritual essence and permits it to enter the physical body. There is a big sign on the drain tile so everyone can understand it: "With God's Help." It works.

One of my students works at a bank. She said Friday had been a very difficult day; she felt that she couldn't take another customer. She suddenly realized that she had been drained of much energy—not only from people, but from the job. She put the "closed" sign on the teller's window, then walked over to the outside window and looked up into the sky. She felt energy come down.

"I had my eyes open and all of a sudden I was radiant," she told me. "I could feel myself tingling. My head went up and my back went straight. I walked back to my desk. I sat there, because it was such a magnificent feeling."

She told this at a meeting, and someone asked her if she became tired again after a while. She said that whenever she felt herself beginning to be drained and whenever she could feel herself going, she experienced a sudden surge of energy. Her head went back, and her back went straight, and she was all right again. She did this several times throughout the day. She said, "It was I, not the Great Spirit, that was draining my energy."

I emphasize, the moment you realize that you have been drained of energy, do something about it; because that is when you *can* do something about it.

Plastic bags work, too. You can put yourself into a bag so

nothing can get at you. You can visualize anything. I used to say in the hospital, "If things get really rough, put yourself in a plastic bag." And nurses would come to me and say, "It really works!"

My grandfather's technique was to look at someone and ask him to sparkle his eyes. This is absolutely the most marvelous way to make your audience and your friends feel great. Sometimes at the start of a lecture, I will say, "Look at your neighbor and make him sparkle!" Then I will say, "Your eyes are the mirror of your soul. When you sparkle your eyes, whether you think you are beautiful or not, you are."

My grandfather would get me agitated and then tell me to sparkle my eyes. I would get so disgusted! I would turn away, but I would always end up looking at him and smiling.

When your situation is draining you of energy, ask yourself these four questions:

Am I happy with the situation? (Obviously, you are not.)

What am I doing to keep the situation alive? Maybe you are not doing a thing, but because you are doing nothing, you are keeping it alive.

What can I do to change the situation?

If I change the situation, how will it affect the other people around me? Does the situation bother other people as it bothers me?

Once the boss went away and left an unfinished job on a desk. He was gone a month. We couldn't use the desk because it was cluttered. Everyone had to walk around the desk, because we were afraid of his wrath. If this was such an important project, it would have been handled before he left. No one touched it. It created a bad situation. When the boss returned, he stormed all over the place because the work hadn't been completed. Yet before he left he had told everyone not to touch the work; he would take care of it when he returned.

This was a classic example of a situation with which no one was happy. So we added to the confusion. No one did anything constructive to bring about peace and contentment. We certainly had fierce thoughts about the boss at the time this was creating confusion.

Every office has something in it that creates confusion. It might just be where the telephone, wastebasket, or desk is situated. It might be something that needs just a little adjustment.

The main thing is that you use your creative self to bring about peace and contentment. It keeps your energy level high. Use the best you have. After you have maintained such a habit, it will work better for you. Never, never try to come up with three or four things to do at once. Take one thing at a time. So, that's about draining energy.

What we have done tonight is to accept the healing forces of the universal spiritual energy that flows through everything and is everywhere. We will close our eyes, and join hands in a circle. Left hand up, right hand down.

The first thing we do now is to think of someone who probably wouldn't necessarily be what we call a friend. Someone whom we wouldn't even care to have as a friend. Now we send thoughts of healing to him. After we have done this, we think of a loved one to whom we will send the healing forces.

We are going to close.

Many moons have traveled the Sky Dome.

Many moons have followed its course.

Many lives have evolved before us, guided by your spiritual force.

The Secret of the Ages is to live in balance, to master all of our inborn talents.

At the close of each day, in thoughts of thanksgiving we reverently say:

Thank you, Great Spirit, for the radiant light that heals each body throughout this night.

7

the
seven worlds

Has civilization on Earth been cyclical? Have there been highly evolved human or hominid cultures before the tradition that led to our epoch? Do memories of glorious times before our own lie half forgotten within man's collective unconscious? Have entire civilizations attained the apex of cultural accomplishment to be crushed during their very golden day to become, a few thousand years later, little more than rumors and twice-told tales. Have mighty empires risen to wax strong and conquer the Earth, only to have their vibrant flames snuffed out in global catastrophes?

It is somehow offensive to contemporary man to consider the thought that a race of prehistoric men may have created a civilization the equal—if not the superior—of his own thousands, even millions, of years ago. Perhaps it is modern man's great pride that inhibits him from taking the time to examine such matters as "lost worlds" with any degree of seriousness.

There is something about the idea of an epoch before our own that seems to ring true in the inner reaches of the human psyche. In his *Worlds in Collision*, Immanuel Velikovsky wondered ". . . to what extent the terrifying experiences of world catastrophes have become part of the human soul and how much, if any, of it can be traced in our beliefs, emotions, and behavior, as directed from the unconscious or subconscious strata of the mind."

Various Amerindian peoples have legends which recount the evolution of mankind through a series of worlds, each of which is destroyed as man forgets the lessons of the Great Spirit and falls away to rely upon his own feeble devices. When this sad state of affairs comes to exist, the Great Spirit causes a time of Great Purification to cleanse the Earth Mother for a new epoch, a new world.

Hopi traditionalists recite their legends of the Four Worlds and warn of their prophecies, which state that a Great Purification will occur when people turn to material, rather than spiritual, matters; when evil ones set out to destroy the land and the life of the Hopi and other Amerindian brothers; when leaders of men turn to evil instead of the Great Spirit; when man has invented something which can fall upon the ground, boil everything within a great area, and turn the land to ashes where no grass will grow.

According to the teachings of the Hopi and many other Medicine people we stand on the very brink of another Great Purification.

I agree with the traditional practitioners of Medicine Power who do not see this time of cleansing as being synonymous with the biblical Judgment Day—the ringing down of the cosmic curtain with a cataclysmic bang and the attendant weeping and gnashing of teeth. From my discussions with Medicine people, it would seem that we also agree that this time of cleansing is the latest in a series of transitional periods which are necessary to man's spiritual evolution. We believe that mankind has been moving higher and higher in the frequency of his spiritual vibration, the raising of his consciousness. The vast majority of Medicine people and New Age visionaries do not see the Great Purification as a time of terrible judgment, but as a time of transcendence.

The legend of the Seven Worlds of the Seneca has been revealed to few outside of those who are a part of the oral tradition of the Iroquois Nation. I am indebted to Twylah Nitsch—both for translating the legend and for permitting me to share it with my readers. She deliberated a great deal before she allowed me to copy the legend from her notebooks. "I agree with you that the time is now," she told me finally. "This must be shared."

To my non-Indian reader, I urge that this account not be read with the superficial superiority of a member of the dominant culture seeking mild diversion from a myth of a quaint, but primitive, people. There is deep symbolism contained within the legend of the Seven Worlds. I can only hope that you will permit yourself to open your spiritual channel and allow the full significance of these words to reach your higher self.

In the mind of Swen-i-o, the Creator, there was no time or place or even human beings—just Swen-i-o, the Creator, and endless space. A world of infinite splendor evolving in total tranquility began in the mind of Swen-i-o, our Creator. Surrounding Swen-i-o was endless space.

The first act of Swen-i-o was to establish a place where all things that were to be born and all things that were to happen could be fulfilled. He named it Eternal Land.

The second act of Swen-i-o was to make a substance that contained the makings of patterns for all things to be created.

The third act of Swen-i-o was to make a substance that floated in a cloud-like maze before his presence. He named this the Field-of-Plenty.

The fourth act of Swen-i-o was to enclose the Field-of-Plenty within a globe where his creations would be manifested. He named this globe the First World.

In the mind of Swen-i-o the First World had been born, and it contained all the limitless creations that were to be. This is where it all began.

The first creation of the First World:
Swen-i-o took the substance from the Field-of-Plenty and arranged a pattern. He threw the substance around and around and caused the first sphere to be born. Swen-i-o breathed around the first sphere to give it power. Breathing upon it filled its spirit. The first sphere floated aloft in the Field-of-Plenty in a brilliant glow of light.

This was the Sun. It was the greatest light, because it was endowed with the greatest gift, the breath of the spiritual life.

The second pattern created by Swen-i-o:
Swen-i-o took the substance from the Field-of-Plenty and arranged a pattern. Rolling the substance around and around caused the second sphere to be born. Swen-i-o breathed upon

the second sphere to give it power. Breathing upon it filled it with the Spirit. The second sphere floated aloft in the Field-of-Plenty in a glow of soft, shimmering light. Swen-i-o named it the Moon. The Moon is different in size because of its power. It is not the same.

The third pattern created by Swen-i-o:

Again Swen-i-o took the substance from the Field-of-Plenty, and rolling the substance around and around, caused the third sphere to be born. He breathed upon the third sphere to give it power. Breathing upon it filled it with the Spirit. The third sphere floated aloft in the Field-of-Plenty in a translucent sheen and was named Water. Water was different from the Sun and the Moon, because its power was not the same.

The fourth pattern created by Swen-i-o:

Again Swen-i-o took the substance from the Field-of-Plenty, and rolling the substance around and around, caused the third sphere to be born. He breathed upon the third sphere to give it power. Breathing upon it filled it with the Spirit. The fourth sphere floated aloft in the Field-of-Plenty in a bronze density, and he named it Earth. Earth is the smallest of the four creations, because its power was not the same. The fourth creation of Swen-i-o received the breath of life.

In the mind of Swen-i-o, the Earth had been divided into four segments, North, South, East, and West, with the colors defined.

Division of the First World:

In the mind of Swen-i-o, the First World would be divided into four segments. Swen-i-o breathed upon the First World, which contained the Sun, Moon, Water, and Earth as it floated in the Field-of-Plenty and caused it to divide into four segments.

Placing the first segment: The first segment was placed by Swen-i-o at the right side of the First World, which was named East, where the sun rises. It was blanketed in the color yellow.

Placing the second segment: The second segment was placed by Swen-i-o at the top of the First World, which was named North, cold. It was blanketed in white.

Placing the third segment: The third segment was placed by Swen-i-o at the left side of the First World, opposite the East. It was named the West, where the sun sets. It was blanketed in the color red.

Placing the fourth segment: The fourth segment was placed in the opposite direction of the North, where it is warm. It was called South, and it was blanketed in darkness.

The decrees of Swen-i-o the Creator:

In the mind of Swen-i-o, the creations of the First World, the Sun, Moon, Water, and Earth, would receive their powers and abilities in decrees. The Sun shall travel the outer rim of the First World in all its brilliant splendor. It shall lift its head, a radiant gold, at a place named the East; passing through the North, a place of total whiteness; to the West, where its golden radiance shall turn to fiery red hues; sinking to rest in a place of total darkness. It was decreed the Sun shall be the Sun Father, whose light and great warmth shall help nourish the creations of the First World. He will be the chief of the Sun tribes (rays), whose light and warmth shall filter down to Earth. These were the first decrees to the Sun in the mind of Swen-i-o.

It was decreed the Moon, the lesser light, will travel the outer rim of the First World, glowing through its shimmering light, passing through the North, a place of total whiteness. The Moon shall send its light rays during the time the Sun rests. It shall manifest four changes upon its face: the new moon; the second moon; the third moon; the full moon, when everything is in full favor. The Moon shall be the chief of the Moon nation (stars). His light shall be the guardian of the night, with starlight trails making paths by a shimmering light. These are the decrees assigned to the Moon in the mind of Swen-i-o.

It was decreed the Water shall float on the First World, reflecting all the colors in the mind of the Creator. Water shall contain the substance in the Field-of-Plenty, where the creatures of the Creator shall evolve upon the Earth. It shall receive the breath of spiritual life, its greatest gift. It shall nurture the creations of the First World. These are the decrees assigned to the Water in the mind of Swen-i-o, the Creator.

It was decreed the Earth shall be the place where the Sun, Moon, and Water shall exert their greatest power. It shall receive gifts and abilities from the Great Spirit. It shall be known as Earth, for on its face all creation shall smile. These are the decrees assigned and fulfilled by Swen-i-o.

Creations of the First World:

In the mind of Swen-i-o the Creator, creatures were to be born, to evolve, and to live in Nature Land. Pattern after pattern was arranged from the substance in the Field-of-Plenty, all endowed with the breath of spiritual life. Taking the substance from the Field-of-Plenty, he sprinkled it throughout Eternal Land, causing its gifts and abilities to be born. Gifts and abilities drifted down from Nature Land to be received by Mother Earth. The Sun smiled on her and sent his rays to filter across her bronze face. In the mind of Swen-i-o, the waters of Nature Land began to evolve. The gifts shared by Mother Earth, nurtured by the power of the Sun and the power of the Water, were responsible for the evolution that led to the manifestation of man.

Migration of the First World:

Man emerged from the deep and walked upon the face of the Earth. He multiplied and established magnificent communities and superb cultures. He was not aware that, during this time, Swen-i-o had taken care of all of his needs, nor was he willing to learn. A very old legend unfolds the happenings that occurred in tracing the development of man from the beginning to his life of perfection.

The First World:

The nations of the First World emerged at the place where the Sun raised its head above the rim of the sky. At this place Mother Earth shared her gifts in great profusion. But the people at that time were not grateful for these gifts and caused a disease of waste to visit Nature Land. Swen-i-o looked at man and arranged a time for the first decree. A silence and great magnitude enveloped the minds of these early people, as a celestial voice spoke: "You are creatures of nature, created by me, to live always in true harmony. Wisdom, if learned, is balance of life. Breaking this law breeds misery and strife. The Great Spirit has spoken."

The people were impressed with the Great Revelation they had heard, and for a time they began to wonder how Nature Land was different. They soon found it very hard to follow the decree of the Great Spirit. As time passed, the decree was forgotten, and Swen-i-o arranged for a cleansing of the First World. He placed a blanket of protection over those creatures who honored his decree. He ordered the Sun to use its power in cleansing the First World. The power of the Sun caused the devastation of the First World.

The dawn of the Second World:

After the Sun's rays penetrated the Earth's surface and destroyed the remnants of the First World, in the mind of Swen-i-o came the dawn of the Second World. The lessons learned from the acts of the people who perished in the First World remained in the minds of those who were saved. Carefully they populated the Second World, and they reaped the benefits from the renewed gifts offered by Mother Earth. Their culture was superb, and it spread rapidly throughout the Second World. Migrations moved toward the North, a place of total whiteness, to the South, a place of total darkness, and with the nations adapting to the environment of these places. Their outer skin became faded where it was cold, and dark where it was hot. Migrations followed the Sun as he traveled the path of the Sky Dome from East to West.

Before long, it became evident that the people of the Second World were following in the footsteps of their predecessors who had inhabited the First World. The wanton waste of the gifts of Mother Earth and the careless imbalance of their lives brought on misery and strife that gripped the world in a disease of destruction. Those who still honored the decree of the Great Spirit were given a blanket of protection, and the cleansing of the Second World was begun.

Swen-i-o ordered the Sun to withdraw its warmth from the face of Mother Earth, leaving only the Moon to exert his power upon Nature Land. The lesser light of the Moon was unable to warm Mother Earth, because its power was not the same as the Sun's. A state of cold settled upon Nature Land. This caused the devastation of the Second World.

The Third World:

The massive cold had completely destroyed the remnants of the Second World. In the mind of Swen-i-o the time came for the dawn of the Third World. The Third World was inhabited by people and creatures with gifts and abilities that surpassed the gifts and abilities of the two previous worlds. They spread their influence along the path of the Sun, establishing magnificent civilizations and cultures, populating more than half of the world. Four races had evolved as a result of migrations: the white, the red, the yellow, and the black—their complexions and physical characteristics having adapted to the environment in which they lived.

During the Third World the four races became more aware of the laws that governed Nature Land, and they made some effort to learn about its mystery. For this reason their civilization flourished for a longer period than the First and Second worlds. But in spite of their knowledge, they became forgetful, and they consistently brought disruption upon the gifts of Mother Earth.

For the third time, those who honored the decree of Swen-i-o were placed under the blanket of protection. Water, the third creation of Swen-i-o, was responsible for the cleansing of the Third World. Since this was in the mind of Swen-i-o, it was done. Water covered the face of Mother Earth. This caused the devastation of the Third World.

In the mind of Swen-i-o came the dawn of the Fourth World:

The migrations of the Fourth World completed the population of the universe from East to West. The greatest span of existence was experienced by the people evolving in the Fourth World, because this world was the Middle World. The environmental experiences of the first three worlds had blended, causing an awakening to visit the minds of the people. Those whose evolvement had reached the awakening period were willing to share their knowledge with others. They began to keep records; but the greatest records were still in the minds of the generations who had lived under the "blanket of protection" and who still honored the decree of the Great Spirit. These people had evolved along the thread that connected them to Swen-i-o, the Creator.

During the Fourth World, the inhabitants became aware of the universal stream that revolved around the world, and they learned the wisdom of enlightenment. It was fully understood how they were evolving and how their spiritual lives guided them in their material existence. Some were aware of the happenings that occurred in the past, and some could even project happenings of the future. Through the minds of these people the Secret of the Ages was recorded.

Unfortunately, too many still pursued the materialistic path, spreading misery and doom among the inhabitants. A dreadful disease plagued the people of the Fourth World. They called it Fear. Its infection caused the nations to search for they-knew-not-what, bringing uncontrolled corruption and strife. For this reason, the cure for this disease was unknown to the inhabitants for a long period of time. More environmental experience and more lessons had to be learned before the disease could be understood. Instead of searching for the cause of the mystery of fear that would bring peace and happiness, they wantonly disrupted the gifts of Mother Earth.

It became evident that the Fourth World would have to undergo a cleansing period to renew the gifts of Mother Earth, just as the three previous worlds had. The cleansing of the Fourth World was exerted by the combined efforts of the Sun, the Moon, and Water upon Mother Earth. The Fourth World's corruption had been the greatest; therefore, her need for renewal, the greatest. The combined powers of the first three creations of Swen-i-o caused the devastation of the Fourth World.

In the mind of Swen-i-o was the dawn of the Fifth World:

The greatest strides in understanding took place in the Fifth World. The era of the awakening had become established, and man found self-satisfaction in sharing his gifts and abilities with others. The Records of the Ages were being uncovered and the false documents of man were being corrected. Man began to understand what he was searching for, and he opened his eyes to the purpose of his life. He searched within himself, and there he was.

The duration of the Fifth World was short compared to the previous worlds. Man had passed through many environmental experiences. His lessons were extremely difficult, but he had achieved self-mastery. He realized that there was much he could do if he used his knowledge to benefit mankind. Heretofore, he had reaped the punishment of destruction only through selfishness. However, he was not yet convinced of the duality of his nature regarding the function of his spiritual mind over the physical body. Wars within his attitudes and thoughts still festered in his mind, creating injustices upon the gifts of Mother Earth.

Man was having difficulty practicing the decree of Swen-i-o that had been revealed in the First World. Repeatedly, there had been messengers of the Great Spirit to remind the people of the wisdom of harmony. Yet they were unable to perpetuate their beliefs after the general disturbances of their way of life in the latter days of the Fourth World. Mother Earth was again in need of a renewal of her gifts. The cleansing was exerted by the power of the Sun and Moon and was completed in the mind of Swen-i-o the Creator. This caused the devastation of the Fifth World.

The dawn of the Sixth World:

The Sixth World had the shortest evolvement period. It was the world that opened the eyes of man. He looked at himself and saw what he really was, but he lacked the ability to change it. He also recognized the necessity of fitting into a pattern that functioned in unison with his world. As yet, he had not fully accepted the laws of nature as his guide. His life at times was still governed by his own selfish thinking. There had to be one more cleansing to renew the gifts of Mother Earth before man truly understood and could practice his purpose in life.

For all six worlds, he had wreaked havoc upon himself,
   his fellow man, and the creatures of Nature.
Now he stood at the threshold of perfection,
   awaiting the wisdom of the ages
   to penetrate his mind.

The cleansing of the Sixth World was exerted by the power

of the Moon, followed by the heating properties of the Water, which paved the way for the dawn of the Seventh World.

The Seventh World:

In the Seventh World, the Happy Hunting Ground,
Man saw beauty everywhere.
He listened to the music of the Universe
And sang his part in the chorus.
He felt love for Swen-i-o and for his fellow man.
He shared his gifts and abilities with others.
He made the Seventh World a place of peace and happiness.

The final cleansing had been completed, and man's life was guided by a spiritual light, the same light that is in the mind of Swen-i-o, the Great Spirit. *Da naho naweh, Swen-i-o!*

Twylah Nitsch's ancestral home on the Cattaraugus Reservation was built in 1858 by her great-grandfather Two Guns. To
the far left is the original Seneca longhouse from the old Buffalo
Creek Reservation. To the far right is Twylah's "doghouse,"
where she often goes for meditation.

Twylah's grandparents, Mr. and Mrs. Moses Shongo.

Twylah.

Twylah with her mother, Maude Shongo Hurd.

Twylah's great ancestor Red Jacket, Seneca chief, military leader, orator.

How Indians prayed: upright, arms outstretched, not with bowed head and bended knee. Painting by Ernie Smith.

Ernie Smith, Seneca Indian artist, who illustrates Twylah's clan stories for children.

Seneca Indian Historical Society Youth Group class in an Amerindian dance. Photo by Joyce Bittner.

This is Twylah's favorite place for going into the Silence. This is where she replenishes her spirit and receives insights from the Great Mystery. While there, she drew Medicine stones from the water for the Steigers and the Steiger children.

De Wayne Wynn holds a jojoba bean, which, as far as has been presently determined, grows only on the San Carlos Apache Reservation. The Apaches have been using the bean for generations to cure blemishes and skin cancer. According to preliminary laboratory tests, jojoba bean oil can be used to replace sperm whale oil in high-performance engines and may have many additional commercial uses.

Chief Eagle in full regalia.

Grandparents of Chief Eagle.

Sun Bear talks of walking in balance.

Sun Bear and Helen.

Left to right: Annie, Wabun, Helen, Richard, Sun Bear, Brad.

The Dakota consider the Black Hills to be the heart of the Earth Mother. "Here, the Indian had everything he needed," Chief Eagle remarked.

Chief Eagle during an interview with Brad Steiger.

8

a revelation
of the pathway
# of peace

Shortly after we had returned from visiting Twylah on the
Cattaraugus Reservation, we received a letter from her stat-
ing that she felt compelled to share with us the symbolical
stepping stones and colors which the Seneca Medicine people had used in the meditative exercise of going into the
Silence. Properly practiced and rightfully employed as a
psychical stimulus, the Pathway of Peace can lead one into
the Great Silence, a spiritual ecstasy far beyond that of
ordinary meditation.

Twylah said that she had spent three days in the Silence,
seeking an answer as to whether the technique should be
shared at this time. She interpreted all the symbols which
came to her as positive assertions that the time was now,

that both Indian and non-Indian were mature enough to receive the lesson and the prayers and to employ them in a respectful and fruitful manner.

She picked up a cassette tape on which to record the Pathway of Peace for mailing to us for transcription. It was not until she had completed an initial taping that she realized that she had recorded over a tape of her mother's voice. She played the tape through, reflected on the words she had recorded, sat for a few moments in reflective silence. Should she have released this material, she wondered. As if in answer to her unspoken question, she was startled to hear her mother's recorded voice saying, "It is good. It is good."

Herewith is *The Pathway of Peace*, a revelation, shared by Twylah Hurd Nitsch:

The Pathway of Peace leads toward peace of mind
The sharing of gifts to every kind
Of creation living upon this earth,
Measuring the steps of each ones' worth.

Seek the trail of Seven Stones
Where Spiritual songs of harmonic tones
Fills the world in harmony,
Soothing throngs of creatures into serenity.

Desire peaks into the soul
Where gifts of life are there to behold
Where charms of peace and harmony
Belong to all for eternity.

We are born into a limited human body into the material world. The search begins for self-knowledge to understand the environment that has so much influence on our personal life-style and personal development. We blend this knowledge to create principles that will guide our material existence. When spiritual awareness filters into our deeper senses, we secure peace and understanding which highlights our personal life-style by permitting us to follow the universal laws and to become attuned with all creation.

This spiritual unfoldment creates a person who lives a life of patience and understanding, who adheres to attitudes that govern his very existence. It shows in the example he lives and his ability to expel fear from his life.

The early Seneca did this by going into the Silence, which followed four steps. The first was the purpose; the second, the preparation; the third, the procedure; the fourth, the progression.

The purpose in life is the learning.
Life is nourished by creative yearning.
With peace and harmony as the goal,
The "Pathway of Peace" is the daily role.

The purpose is to establish a personal routine for entering into the Silence that will become a regular experience in spiritual enrichment in one's life-style.

The preparation is arranged for this solitary ritual as one would prepare for his daily intake of food, in order to satisfy the hunger for spiritual growth. We think of it as the spiritual nourishment that furnishes the lifeline, as well as the guideline, for our very existence. By preparing in this way, we can secure greater success.

The procedure is to open the way for the spiritual forces

to enter within the physical body through self-awareness.
The procedure is called "Rekindling the Spiritual Light."
Thoughts that fill the mind are:

A glorious beam
Drifts throughout my body
Drenching me with its Essence Supreme.

The Light of all Light,
The Spirit of all love,
The Source of all knowledge and inspiration,
The Source of all creation—
Of time, of place, of thoughts, of sound,
Of Life-profound!

All voices sing-out in thoughts of thanksgiving
For the gifts of talents and abilities in communicating
Through expressions in sound, in sight, in scent,
In taste, in touch, in awareness, and in all emotions,
The Spiritual Revelations!

The progression:
There comes a time in everyone's life when becoming a
seeker draws the individual closer to the spiritual self. The
Seneca call this "approaching the first stone," or the "pathway
of self-knowledge."
Seven stepping stones mark the trail that leads the seeker
into the Great Silence.

An outstretched hand, four fingers and a thumb
Symbolic of life, unity, equality, and eternity
Guides the seeker along the "Pathway of Peace"
And the journey has begun.

The first stepping stone, the Blood-stone, glows in radiant shades of red. It plants the seed that awakens the seeker to the spiritual way of faith and beckons the seeker to the entrance of the Pathway of Peace.

The Blood-stone has seven facets. Each facet designates one of the spiritual senses of sound, sight, scent, taste, touch, awareness, and emotions. Standing upon the first stone is symbolic of the life materialized in the physical world and is a daily venture in faith.

The seeker learns that the Great Mystery, the Spiritual Essence, is connected with all things in creation and that all things in creation are connected with one another. It is the impressions influenced by this interconnection that affect the experiences in all creation.

The radiance of the Blood-stone flows throughout the seeker and into the material world, uniting all creation into thoughts and feelings of faith.

Becoming aware of the existence of the first stepping stone and the lessons it imparts opens the way to the second stepping stone on the Pathway of Peace.

The second stepping stone, the Sun-stone, glows in radiant shades of yellow. It plants the seed that awakens the seeker to the spiritual way of love, and it beckons the seeker to dwell upon the Sun-stone on the Pathway of Peace.

The Sun-stone has the same seven facets that designate the powerful spiritual senses of sound, sight, scent, taste, touch, awareness, and emotions. Standing upon the Sun-stone is symbolic of the life materialized in the physical world and is a daily venture in love.

Its radiance of love flows throughout the seeker and into the material world. Faith and love go hand in hand. It is the spiritual expression of faith and love that makes the world go around and helps the seeker to grow in peace and harmony.

Becoming aware of the existence of the Sun-stone and the lessons it imparts opens the way to the third stepping stone on the Pathway of Peace.

The third stepping stone, the Water-stone, glows in radiant shades of blue. It plants the seed that awakens the seeker to the spiritual way of cleansing and soothing, and it beckons the seeker to dwell upon the Water-stone.

The Water-stone has seven facets. Each facet designates one of the spiritual senses of sound, sight, scent, taste, touch, awareness, and emotions.

Standing upon the Water-stone is symbolic of the life materialized in the material world and is a daily venture of cleansing and being soothed.

The radiance of the Water-stone flows throughout the seeker and into the material world, nourishing it with cleansing purity. It is the fluid property that unites all creation into the stream of spirituality and helps the seeker grow toward peace and harmony through its expression of peaceful relaxation.

Becoming aware of the existence of the Water-stone and the lessons it imparts opens the way to the fourth stepping stone on the Pathway of Peace.

The fourth stepping stone, the Fertility-stone, glows in radiant shades of green. It plants the seed that awakens the seeker to the spiritual way of abundance and renewal, and it beckons the seeker to dwell upon the Fertility-stone.

The Fertility-stone has seven sides, each designating one of the spiritual senses of sound, sight, scent, taste, touch, awareness, and emotions.

Standing upon the Fertility-stone is symbolic of the life materialized in the material world and is a daily venture in physical and natural growth. Its radiance flows throughout the seeker and into the material world, nourishing it with abundant life.

It is the renewing properties of the fourth stepping stone that unites all creation into environmental awareness and helps the seeker grow toward peace and harmony.

Becoming aware of the existence of the Fertility-stone and the lessons it imparts opens the way to the fifth stepping stone on the Pathway of Peace.

The fifth stepping stone, the Blossoming-stone, glows in radiant shades of coral pink. It plants the seeds that awaken the seeker to the spiritual way of upliftment, and it beckons the seeker to dwell upon the fifth stepping stone on the Pathway of Peace. The Blossoming-stone has the same powerful facets as the previous stepping stones.

The radiance of its unfolding properties flow throughout the seeker and into the material world, nourishing it with beauty and spiritual insight.

Standing upon the Blossoming-stone is symbolic of the life materialized in the physical world. It offers a daily venture in intuitive impulses and is a gift received on the Pathway of Peace.

Its properties of upliftment help the seeker grow toward peace and harmony.

Becoming aware of the existence of the Blossoming-stone and the lessons it imparts opens the way to the sixth stone on the Pathway of Peace.

The sixth stepping stone, the Charity-stone, glows in a radiant burst of spiritual light. It plants the seed that awakens the seeker to the spiritual way of benevolence in thoughts and deeds, and it beckons the seeker to dwell upon the sixth stepping stone on the Pathway of Peace.

The Charity-stone has the same powerful facets as the stepping stones that preceded it.

The radiance of the Charity-stone flows throughout the seeker and into the material world, nourishing it with acts of kindness and understanding.

It is the charitable properties of the sixth stepping stone that unite all creation into the ways of Spiritual Harmony. Its brilliance crystallizes the highest spiritual self in preparation for entering into the Great Silence.

Becoming aware of the sixth stepping stone and the lessons it imparts opens the way to the seventh stepping stone on the Pathway of Peace.

The seventh stepping stone, the Healing-stone, glows in radiant shades of lavender. It plants the seed that awakens the seeker to the spiritual way of healing—the highest creative spirituality. It beckons the seeker to dwell on the seventh stepping stone on the Pathway of Peace.

The radiance of the Healing-stone projects the powerful facets in sound, in sight, in scent, in taste, in touch, in awareness, and in emotions, and it flows into the seeker and into the material world, nourishing all creation with the Essence of Spiritual Healing that leads toward peace and harmony.

The healing properties unite all creation into spiritual attunement, which flows throughout Eternity.

Becoming aware of the existence of the seventh stepping stone leads to the threshold of the Great Silence that opens the way of Spiritual Peace and Harmony.

In the Silence
All creation unites and communicates
The Spiritual Way.
Where life is pure, life is fulfilling;
Life is understanding; life is sharing;
Life is abundant; life is unity; and
Life is Eternity.
The ecstasy of Spiritual Enlightenment.

As the seeker descends the Pathway of Peace—

The seventh stepping stone reveals Spiritual Healing.
The sixth stepping stone reveals Spiritual Charity.
The fifth stepping stone reveals Spiritual Insight.
The fourth stepping stone reveals Spiritual Awareness.
The third stepping stone reveals Spiritual Cleansing.
The second stepping stone reveals Spiritual Love.
The first stepping stone reveals Spiritual Faith.

The Light of all Light,
The Light of all Faith and Love,
The Light of all Knowledge and Inspiration,
The Source of all Creation—
The Spiritual Revelation.

9

dallas chief eagle
—spiritual warrior
of the sioux

"A cowboy and an Indian die and go to heaven. They get met by St. Peter at the pearly gates, and St. Pete ushers the cowboy into a Cadillac. The angels come out and they line the streets. They start to cheer and the cowboy is driven down between the rows of angels while they stand there applauding and tossing confetti, ticker tape, streamers. The Indian is given an old Model-T that can just barely sputter. By the time the old clunker reaches the parade route, nearly all the angels have gone home.

"The Indian is a little upset. 'I had to take all that abuse on earth,' he grumbles. 'Now when I go to heaven, I get the same treatment. The cowboy is up front in the Cadillac, and I'm in the back in an old Model-T.'

"St. Peter takes the Indian aside, puts an arm around him, and says, 'You must understand. We are pleased to have you in heaven, but, you see, this is the first cowboy we've ever had!'"

Dallas Chief Eagle uses humor a great deal, both in his lectures and in his day-to-day dealings with his white and red brothers. He learned long ago that humor can disguise hurt and pain and transform them into effective teaching points. When Chief Eagle takes the old "cowboy-and-Indian" motif so familiar to anyone who has grown up in a nation of Saturday matinées, cap pistols, and Manifest Destiny and combines it with the whiteman's religious hope of a reward on the "other side," he manages to take two of the dominant culture's cherished symbols and turn them around to make a joke on the whiteman.

Humor also permits Chief Eagle to juxtapose past and present and to offer guidance for the future.

"There was this time when I was supposed to speak on this campus. When I arrived, I found it embroiled in the protests of activist students. And here I am supposed to speak about the redman and his problems. I decided to change my lecture format, and I called right away for questions from the audience.

"Right away, a young woman asks, 'What do you think about the invasion of Cambodia? Do you think the United States will continue its invasion, or do you think that the U.S. will stop, as it has promised?'

"I answered, 'Miss, I think the United States will be like the rapist who says, "Don't worry, ma'am. I'll just go in an inch!"'"

From this springboarding off the present, Chief Eagle

could return to the past. He could delineate how so very often, in treaty violation after treaty violation, the whiteman told the Indian, "Don't worry. We're just going to take a little bit more of your land."

As Chief Eagle told this story, I could envision him living at the time of his great ancestor Crazy Horse. I could visualize him employing the same wit, the same powers of persuasive oratory which he possesses today. I could hear him saying to the assembled council:

"The whiteman has invaded our sacred Black Hills. These hills are to have been protected by treaty from the whiteman forever. But now he has found the yellow gold that he holds so dear, and he tells us that he will enter our hills for only a little distance. Brothers, I say that the whiteman's promise is like that of the rapist who tells the woman he plans to violate, 'Don't worry, ma'am, I will only go in an inch!'"

Dallas Chief Eagle does not live in the buffalo-hide teepees of his Lakota (Sioux) ancestors. He lives with his family in a small, modest home in Pierre, South Dakota. His life is now in the city, where he is director of tourism for the Development Corporation of the United Sioux Tribes of South Dakota. His wife, Shirley, a Brule Sioux, together with the daughters still at home, offer Dallas Chief Eagle both a happy home life and the inspiration to gain the most advantages from the System that he can for his people.

The Chief Eagle residence, just two blocks off the end of main street in Pierre, harbors most of the mid-America trappings of any other home in the city. Kids and their friends sprawl in front of after-school television. Comfortable furniture made for living and using issues unspoken invitations to sit down and relax. A statue of the Virgin Mary stands on a mirrored cabinet. A large drum rests in a corner of the dining room. Medicine articles and Chief Eagle's own inspired Medicine paintings hang here and there about the house. The home, like its owner, reflects a blending of traditional Amerindian culture and Medicine Power with twentieth-century, mid-American aspirations.

Pierre is the capital of South Dakota. The town is laid out in typical Midwestern style, with shop buildings lining either side of a main street. Western Americana is evident in the shops, supermarkets, Western wear stores, and taverns, but there appears to be no aggressive effort to capitalize on the cowboy flavor. Most of the men wear boots and cowman-style hats, although the appeal of Western-cut suits and sport coats seems to have become minimal. The people are Midwestern-friendly, and they like to go for coffee to chat and to tease one another. Omnipresent posters for a LeRoy Van Dyke concert indicates that country-Western music best tells the stories of the people's loves, sorrows, and triumphs; but the radio stations offer a mixture of country, hard rock, and soft rock, bubble-gum music.

Dave Graham, a friend and business associate, and I stopped for breakfast in a small town outside of Pierre. The tiny restaurant in which we ate was obviously a town gathering place. Several men sat at a table, warming up to the frosty day with coffee and a dice game.

A short, stocky rancher stomped up to the men and earnestly began to encourage them to attend a meeting that night which would plan certain moves to bolster meat prices for the producer.

A large man growled, "Why the hell should a sheepman like me do anything to help a cowpuncher like you?"

The question might have come from a dozen Western movies and served as the preamble to a fistfight, but the year was 1973, not 1873. "Because," the short rancher answered, refusing to be intimidated by either his adversary's size or his question, "we are both meat producers. You are going to help us and we are going to help you, because we are in the same boat! Together, we can make some noise."

The situation was more than a hundred years old, but the political aspects of its solution were very contemporary.

South Dakota, with its blend of traditional and modern trappings, its echoes of the past seeking to retain volume against the cacophony of today, seemed like an appropriate place to be discussing Medicine Power of the traditional Amerindian and its application and practice in the Space-Aged 1970s.

Many years ago, Dallas Chief Eagle made a promise to himself that he would write a book about the Sioux that would be as culturally authentic and as historically accurate as he could make it. In 1967 *Winter Count* (Johnson Publishing, Boulder, Colorado) appeared. Chief Eagle wrote the book six times in four years, working at night after he had completed his regular shift at a steel mill. In addition to his credit as a novelist, Chief Eagle is also an accomplished painter who specializes in Amerindian scenes.

In a special ceremony held in October 1967 the Teton Sioux elected Dallas Bordeaux their chief. The great chief Red Cloud was named to the title in 1868, and when he died, his people chose not to select a new chief out of respect to the wise leader and skilled military strategist. Chief Red Cloud defeated the United States troops in every major en-

counter and won all the treaty concessions he demanded.
To succeed Red Cloud is a great honor.

A feast and a powwow were held, and Chief Eagle was presented with Red Cloud's pipe, which bears 112 notches on
it for the number of Indians, soldiers, and settlers personally
killed by the war chief during his lifetime. A number of Indians cited Chief Eagle's past accomplishments, including his
novel *Winter Count*. A restricted number of elders were present at the ceremony. Edgar Red Cloud and Charlie Red
Cloud sponsored Chief Eagle. The matron of honor was
Alice Black Horse. Frank Fools Crow, the ceremonial chief,
conferred the honor. The Bureau of Indian Affairs does not
officially recognize Dallas Chief Eagle as chief of the Tetons,
choosing, rather, to regard the title as honorary.

Since Chief Eagle's wife, Shirley, is descended from the
famous Brule chief Spotted Tail, it should hardly be sur-
prising to learn that the two of them long ago decided to rear
their children in a combination of modern, midstream North
American culture and Amerindian traditionalism. At the
same time that he is a devout student of nature according to
the ancient philosophy of the Amerindian, Dallas Chief Eagle is also a practicing Roman Catholic. Chief Eagle is a
syncretist. He believes in blending—in one practice and philosophy drawing from another.

"I have delved deeply into the ways of my ancestors," he
said. "I know that there is great wisdom and good in Indian
theology. I have never believed that Christianity has a fran-
chise on religion. Wisdom is God-given, and you can get it
only through the study of nature.

"So it is in the material aspects of life. In order to generate
interest in the products of the American Indian, we have to

use the whiteman's method of promotion. White technology should be applied to producing Indian goods. We need both cultures. We should not try to destroy one another. We do not have to merge or integrate, but we can learn to take the good from each and apply it to our modern life."

What would be the most common symbol for the Great Spirit among the Lakota?

DALLAS CHIEF EAGLE: There is no symbol as such for the Great Spirit. The closest would be the symbol of peace, the pipe or the crossed pipes, with the stem upward.

Would wakan *be the best word in Lakota for the Great Mystery?*

Wakan means holy, sacred.

Some authorities say that wakan is the word for the Great Spirit, but it seems that the translation of "Great Mystery" or "an essence that permeates all life" would be better.

Yes, because the Indian never sat around trying to figure out what the Great Spirit looked like.

We pay homage to this Great Spirit, or Great Mystery, through his own creations—the Sun, the Earth, the wind, the thunder, the lightning. The earth must not be spoiled by the men who worship in mere lodges, by the arrogance of those who have never known defeat, by the self-righteousness of those who violate treaties and punish those who would resist such violations.

As we stand uneasily in the border country of the Atomic Age, we have set our feet on spiritual pathways which may thrust us against furies of nature and man which can overpower us as unsympathetically as the blue-coated cavalry overpowered the Sioux. Instead of courage and determination, we have developed productivity and comfort. These may be our undoing. Whether one lives as a Sioux or a middle-class American, he can find his highest ideals subverted to savagery and greed.

The Great Mystery made nature for us to use and preserve, but nature also imposes obligations upon us. We are only passing through life on our way to the Spirit World of our ancestors.

We Indians must pray to the Holy Mystery and ask that some day the whitemen will better understand us, that the needs of their consciousness will awake and grow. Our freedom is our way of life, but to others, it could be a different thing. You have to know what you are in order to feel the Great Spirit in nature. It is only through nature that one can gain communion with the Holy Mystery.

You have expressed so much of yourself and Indianness in Winter Count. *Are you able to utilize your paintings in the same dual role of self-expression and teaching?*

I think so. The early Indian sensed the beauty of nature and expressed it in art. My forefathers made storytelling pictographs, which led to abbreviated picture-writing. Some present-day artists use a conglomeration of abbreviated pictures combined into one scope and tab it modern art. I am certain my ancestors would disagree violently with this kind of painting.

As an Indian artist, I seek to express myself through the past and through tradition, which is interwoven with Indian theology. The early Indian artists who worked with crude tools and simple pigments left proof that great art does not necessarily relate to the so-called intellectual attainments of civilization. Great art rises from basic human emotions and is timeless.

In my opinion, modern abstract art is immoral. It is a selfish restriction of a God-given resource. It is a camouflage. It is like putting a cloak over something that would otherwise be beautiful.

Chief Eagle, let us talk about your personal background. You know, all the vital statistics.

I was born in 1925 in a tent on the Rosebud Reservation. That tent wasn't an Indian teepee; it was a Montgomery Ward tent. I was orphaned as a child, and according to our culture, the eldest of the tribe are to raise the orphans.

Those who brought me up taught me not to accept the non-Indian ways of life. They would not even let me learn English. To them, everything was temporary. Such a belief can be traced back to their history. The Lakota were nomads. They never had a permanent place to live. Even if some marauding tribe were to conquer them, this would be only a temporary condition. So when the big European invasion came, they regarded it as a temporary condition. They knew the old ways would come back. This is why they taught me that it was useless to learn the whiteman's life-style.

I had quite an experience on my first day of school. I reluctantly went with the agency police and a Jesuit missionary to the mission school.

Why were the police there?

To make certain that I stayed in school! I was five, six years old. I didn't speak English; I knew only Sioux people.

Anyway, my experience came with the language. A nun was teaching us English, and I couldn't understand a word she was saying. I couldn't respond to anything she said. She finally grabbed me by the elbows and stood me up in the middle of the aisle. She jabbered some more, took me by the arm, and led me to a corner, where she set me on a stool and put a long, pointed cap on my head.

I was a very proud little boy. The way I had been raised had conditioned me to accept that any type of commendation, any type of decoration, any honor would be conferred on the head. I thought to myself, here it is my first day at the whiteman's school, and already I have been recognized as a superior little boy. I have been given a fine headdress.

Then, at recess time, my classmates told me that I was wearing a dunce cap. I was being punished for not being able to speak English.

I suppose most whites would be surprised to learn that many Indian children on the reservations do not speak English until they are exposed to the public, or mission, schools. How many Indians would you say are bilingual?

In this last half of the twentieth century, I would say about one fourth are bilingual. In my opinion, this is very unfortunate. There is a great deal of knowledge to be gained from the Indian language.

Wisdom does not come from institutions. It comes from a higher power. We do not identify this higher power as a human being. We do not identify it as any one particular energy or life. The higher power, the Great Mystery, is identified by all energies in life. The Great Mystery is in a blade of grass, an animal, a fowl, the thunder, or a rock.

Most of the Sioux west of the Missouri are Tetons, which comprises over three fourths of the Sioux tribes. We use the "l" not the "d" when we speak. Lakota not Dakota. I fear our young people are losing a great deal of their culture and their heritage. They don't try to learn Indian from their elders. I think this is a great loss to America and to the system.

How would you compare English and Lakota in terms of effectiveness of communication?

I have never really given this much thought. I would say that Russian would be fairly easy for a Lakotan to learn because of their pronunciations. In my trips to Japan I have found that many of their words have the same pronunciations, but entirely different meanings.

I have always been quite amazed by the fact that the Jews called God "Jahweh." I think of the Passover, of the Jews bloodying the doorposts. In Sioux, Jahweh means "to make the levy."

When I joined the U.S. Marines in 1942, I had to fill out a questionnaire. It asked, "What foreign language do you speak?" I put down "English." The Marine Corps papers made a big thing of it, but I was serious.

Was the school you attended a boarding school?
Yes.

What do you think it does to the heads of Indian kids to be educated in that kind of environment?

I think it is complete isolation. I didn't get used to it until I was fourteen years old. If you want to look at things from a humane point of view, the reservations themselves are really set up as stockades. Boarding school was just a little step from the stockade environment into restrictiveness. Boarding schools take you away from people. I don't think this is very educational.

They have changed the system since then, and I am very glad. Even though an Indian child may not know a word of English until he comes to school, his IQ is equal to that of any other American child. When an Indian child goes to school, however, right around fourth or fifth grade, he begins to realize that he is a very different person.

What causes that realization?

The things that he is taught have no relevance to his way of life. There is nothing in the textbooks about the great chiefs, the great warriors, the spiritual principles of Indianness. And the books talk about dad going to work in a taxi, getting in an elevator and being taken to his executive offices in a skyscraper. This way of life has no relevance to the Indian child. These things are phenomenal to him.

Why does it take until the fourth or fifth grades for this realization to occur?

That is the way the curriculum is set up. Before those grades, the Indian kid thinks, "I am just a kid like these other guys." But then the teachings of the whiteman start to show him that he is out of the circle. He begins to lose his sense of belonging. He starts looking around him, and he sees everything—the teacher, his classmates, even the movies he sees —telling him that he is a different kind of person.

Then in about the fifth grade he starts reading in his history book how the great heroes and military leaders of the last century did their best to solve the terrible Indian problem for the United States by annihilating as many tribes as possible.

Right then the Indian kid realizes, "Hey, these people are really down on me!" He gets this feeling of being dispossessed. Maybe a year or two later, this psychological depression and alienation builds in him to the breaking point. Then we experience increased absenteeism. Maybe in seventh or eighth grade, he drops out. Maybe he waits until high school.

The Indian child is confused. He believes that he doesn't

belong. He knows only that the System regards him as an underling. He sees nothing which indicates that the System is interested in him or wants to help him. There is no way that a whiteman can really understand the psychological impact that reservation life can have on an Indian child.

Let me give you an example. Let us say that the Communist Chinese come to Decorah, Iowa, where you live. They tell you that they have conquered the United States and that you are now their prisoner. You haven't got a thing to worry about, they say, because they have worked out an agreement, a treaty, between the Chinese people and the American people. The Chinese will now feed, clothe, and educate you. Pretty nice, huh? All your needs will be taken care of. Of course, you don't own anything now. The Chinese will confiscate your bank accounts, your cars, your homes.

Then one day they say, Decorah is no longer to be your home. Chinese immigrants wish to settle there. You will be moved to an arid piece of land. No more beautiful trees, trout streams, and green grass, Brad. Decorah belongs to the Chinese. That miserable piece of land over there is yours.

But again they tell you, don't worry. The land does not need to be green and fertile. They will feed you; they will clothe you; they will provide for your every need. But now they don't want you or your kids to speak English any more. You will speak only Chinese or you will be punished severely. And the clothes? From now on, it will be only Chinese-style pajama clothing. Food? No more meat and potatoes. From now on, rice and slivers of raw fish is what is good for you. And get rid of those knives and forks! Civilized people eat with chopsticks.

Of course your children need to read and to write—Chinese. And the history books now emphasize the glories of the Chinese people, concentrating upon the period after the advent of Marxism in their country. White leaders are made to appear as buffoons and evil men.

And your religious practices must go! No more of this brain-softening Christianity. Forget your religions and memorize the teachings of Chairman Mao.

I am getting the picture very vividly, Chief Eagle.

Well, now you see that even though all your physical needs may be well provided for by another people, you can be left with nothing. Psychological destruction is one of the most terrible things that you can do to a human being.

Do you feel that reservations have been little more than prisoner-of-war camps?

From the traditional Indian point of view, in a prisoner-of-war camp, you have hope. You know that someday the war will end. On the reservations, there is no hope.

Is the school system on the Rosebud Reservation today more like that of mainstream American society?

Right now it is moving that way. The missionary schools have been converted to day schools. There is no boarding school. In other South Dakota communities, there are Indians and non-Indians serving together on school boards, and the kids mix together. This gives them all a sense of belonging. It is a shame that it had to take a century for the whiteman to realize some of these things.

Red Cloud himself wanted education for his people. He made several trips to Washington to plead for teachers. He received only negative responses until his last trip, when some Jesuits took notice of his plea. They established Holy

Rose Mission, and even though about four years ago the name of the school was changed to Red Cloud Indian School, most Indians still refer to the institution as Holy Rose.

I hear so often of Indian youths involved in court cases because they have refused to cut their long, Indian-style hair.

The long hair helps to build pride. You cannot motivate people until they have developed their sense of pride. These kids are desperately searching for identity. They figure that, under the new civil rights rulings, they can at least exercise the external appearance aspect of their traditionalism.

These kids are learning to be active, and that is good in a democratic system. Activism makes the white people take notice. You have to take care of a squeak in the wheel, whether or not the noise comes from a minority. The white-man founded this country on revolutionary tactics. I think the Indians taking over the offices of the Bureau of Indian Affairs in Washington is parallel to the Boston Tea Party. If you want to change this System, believe me, you have to use an ax to gain attention. That is the only way you can make this System readjust itself to become more responsive to those it governs.

Are there any other personal memories of your early educational experience that you would like to share?

Well, yes, maybe it is time we had a smile. This same nun who grabbed me and punished me with a dunce cap because I did not know how to speak English always used to walk around the classroom with one of these metal frog clickers. You know what I mean? Those things you press with thumb and forefinger to make them go "click-clack."

She would say, "Class, put away your books [click-clack!]." "Class [click-clack!], it is time for recess." "Class, pick up your pencils and papers and get back to work [click-clack!]." She really had us regimented. She was a very strict disciplinarian, yet we knew that she represented God on earth, in spite of that frog clicker in her hand.

One day she gave us an assignment in art. We were to draw our conception of what God looked like. As I told you —and as you well know—such a project is totally alien to the Indian theology; but we were learning to think like white children.

I had my catechism on my desk, and it had a picture of Jesus on the cover. I figured that since Jesus was the son of God, God must look like an older Jesus. So I used that as my model and handed in my assignment. I fared pretty well. But the poor little girl next to me really got a scolding and got set in a corner. She drew a picture of God as a giant frog.

Here is a poem that I have written about myself:

In an Indian tent he was born.
In a crowded school he was alone.
In a modern world his legs would bend.
Only on canvas and paper he lives his heritage.

I think that gives a pretty good poetic word-picture of how I see myself. Here is another, more general, portrait of the Amerindian:

THE ROCKY MOUNTAIN INDIAN

The center of this land was my home,
A rainbow country flung high by the Great Spirit,
Where the earth meets the playground of clouds and
    thunder.

Its highest peaks veiled with the haze of the starland,
Like teepees in the sky, fashioned by Spirit hands,
They loom as unchallenged monuments of earth.

None of the bow and arrow tell of this high empire,
Where the roving winds bow to its granite forms,
With lakes like random robes upon the council floor
Lay mirroring nature with peaceful meditation.
Reflected, too, are the frowning walls of jagged cliffs
Its heights held hostage to the turbulent streams.

Once forest tongues spoke in nature's dialect,
Where animals played in the hallowed realms of green,
Where the haunting calls of love-flutes made envy.
And tom-toms vibrated in the aspen plots, as dancing
black-haired children laughed and sang,
Their voices heard over the noisy foamed-rivers.

Then from the dawn country came the new noise of strife,
crushing the things of the spirit with alarm.
The land now echoed with shouts and curses of greed
The alien needs rang high in authority to destroy a creed
of ancient rights and legends.
The palefaces' hunt was on.

Werewolves began to split the stillness of the forest.
The air was choked with laws of different moods and
    minds;
The smoking mystery irons pushed down the tomahawks.
Anguished grief-chants condensed through the night.
Like the big freeze, icy resentment tortured the native
    man,
Leaving him little room to stand.

Famine began to stalk the teepees of the Rocky Moun-
tains,
pushing scarred and unbowed heads to the flatlands.
Brute passion ruled the invaders' minds and hands.
A sad change came to the land of the Rockies.
Now only the solemn spruce stands wake over my ances-
tors.
The paleface came to stay.

How did you and the U.S. Marine Corps get along?

I was in the Marine Corps from 1942 until I was discharged
in October of 1945. All I can say is that with General Mac-
Arthur's help, I won the war in the Southwest Pacific.

You can check this out: The highest percentage of all the
volunteers in World War I, World War II, Korea, and Vietnam come from the American Indians. I asked an aunt of
mine which branch of service I should enter, and she said I
would really look beautiful in a Marine Corps uniform. I was
sad that she died when I was overseas, and she never did see
me in my uniform.

I filled one pocket with Indian bread—or "cowboy bread"
as non-Indians call it—and hitch-hiked to Rapid City, the
nearest place where I could join the Marine Corps. I spoke
to this sergeant, and he gave me a bunch of papers. He told
me to fill them out, and they would call me in a month or so.
I told him that I didn't think I could live that long! So he
put me up in a hotel that night and the following day he sent
me off to Minneapolis to take my physical.

The Marine Corps gave me some problems, but not like
you would think. I was given some pretty tough assignments,

because my superiors reasoned that since I was an Indian, I would make a good scout.

"Go out there and track the enemy down," they'd say, "then shoot some tracer bullets at them so your squad will know where they are."

The trouble is, when you let these bullets go, the enemy knows where *you* are, too! I would shoot the tracers, then run like hell for another spot to crouch.

Here were the good old stereotypes again. The officers took it for granted that I was the same caliber of warrior that my ancestors were.

Was it back to Rosebud after the war was over?

I went back and finished my high school. Then I went to Chicago and took some specialized courses. I went to Oklahoma A & M and to Tulsa City College. I also attended the University of Idaho at Pocatello.

I was a laborer for a long time. When I went to college, I was the best janitor on the job. I have been an industrial engineer and an industrial relations man for a steel corporation. I was a public relations man for H. L. Hunt for two years. I worked as a main negotiator for the United States Steel workers and as a financial secretary for them.

After representing all those thousands of steel workers and their families, being their negotiator and agreements man, serving sometimes as their priest, I got to thinking about going back to my people and helping them. All my life I have felt that I had a role to fulfill. I still feel that I am not quite in my proper role. I know that I have a commitment that I can't quite identify as yet. The mystics, the Yuwipi people, tell me that a more important role is coming for me to fulfill.

Could that role be to devote yourself full time to Medicine work?

I do not know that I am worthy. Look at me; I smoke too much for one thing. I practice Medicine, but there are so many administrative tasks that I feel I must do for my people.

You know, Indian Medicine, Indian theology, involves a great deal of what we now call parapsychology. Whenever I come to visit our holy men, they are always waiting for me. They always know when I will come.

I have seen these holy men bathe their hands in liquid prepared from boiling herbs and be able to place their hands in flames with impunity. I have seen a wise man drink a tea for three days and be able to read my thoughts as specifically as I read a book. I have tried to jumble my thoughts and confuse him when he does this, but I have never succeeded in distracting him from accuracy.

For the present, then, it would seem that you consider yourself an activist, as opposed to the full shamanistic role wherein you would withdraw a bit more from materialistic concerns.

I am more of an activist now, that is true. But the Yuwipi men have asked me to develop the mystical part of my life more than I have.

Perhaps right now, you might be classified as a warrior-mystic, such as your ancestor Crazy Horse was.

Yes, I am a mystic, but I must now fight for Indian causes. And I am definitely an activist. I feel, however, that one does not have to bend over toward radicalism or even revolutionary means. I think Dr. Martin Luther King with his example and his work did more for the Indians and other minority groups than Lincoln, Roosevelt, the Kennedys, or anyone.

Do you combine Roman Catholicism and traditionalism to practice Medicine Power?

I am more of a traditionalist, but I do live a bicultural existence.

I like the term acculturation a lot better than assimilation or integration, because when you assimilate or integrate, you have to give up your Indianism. You have to take what the dominant society demands.

I think I have mastered the art of bicultural livelihood. I think the educational institutions should take a closer look at what they are teaching and recognize that one does not have to give up his Indianism to learn how to master a livelihood acceptable to the dominant society.

I could be 100 per cent Indian, as far as culture is concerned. Tomorrow I could go down to the reservation and be 100 per cent Indian. Today, I am sitting here with you like an average, middle-class man.

I am bilingual; I am bicultural; and as far as my religion is concerned, I am also a "bi." My faith in Indian theology is equally as strong as my faith in Christianity. I rely on faith. I see a lot of things wrong with Christianity, but I can live with it. At the same time, I am not about to let a lot of my Indian religion go, because I value its principles higher than Christianity's dogmas and doctrines. I am "bi," and I feel absolutely no conflict at all.

Within the current revival of the Amerindian's spiritual heritage are a number of native Americans who feel that they must go back to the ways their forefathers worshiped, that they must go back to the ways that the Great Spirit intended. Other Amerindians say that Apostolic Christianity—Christianity minus its multitude of dogmas—and Amerindian tra-

ditionalism are very close, and they see where it is possible for the two to blend. Would you agree with this kind of syncretism?

I certainly do. The movement of Christianity has become twisted because man has interjected too much into its spiritual flow. Dogmas! How can any man say what the Great Spirit thinks? The Supreme Power gives man a message, sets an example. The Great Mystery sets forth guidelines. If man puts forth any dogma or doctrine, I think he has put forth a challenge to the Great Spirit.

You would always hold your own visions above any dogma?

Definitely, because that vision comes from the Great Spirit to me. I think it would be an insult to the Great Mystery to discard his message in favor of following one of his creation's dogmas.

Have you ever been accused of reinforcing white stereotypes of the Indian because you practice such "superstitions" as Medicine Power?

Let those who mock Medicine practice experience it. You know, we Indians were advanced in our social customs, as well as our spiritual expression when the Great Invasion came to our shores.

The women of today are asking for equality. The American Indians had equality. Women served on our councils. Women played a very influential part in the affairs of a tribe, band, or clan. During the Great Invasion, the whitemen would not deal with our Indian women leaders. Even in the treaty affairs, they would not deal with our Indian women leaders. They excluded them from the meetings.

The whiteman came and destroyed many things for us.

The whiteman was in his puberty then. There still are not many who have matured.

I deal with Medicine Power with the utmost respect and seriousness. To inform modern man that Medicine Power exists and has great relevance for today's society, in my opinion, surely does not put the Amerindian down or reinforce white stereotypes of the superstitious Indian.

A whiteman can wear an expensive business suit, drive an expensive car to work in an electronically dominated office, and practice the religious concepts outlined two thousand years ago by a carpenter's son from Nazareth. That whiteman, who considers himself a child of the Space Age, would resent any implication that he was superstitious because he bent his knee to receive the body and blood of a man long dead on a cross.

In my opinion, the spiritual life encompasses those things which are universal, which are constant. If one chooses to regard any form of spiritual expression as superstition, that may be his intellectual opinion, the path he has elected to walk. But no one has the right to decree one religious expression sacrosanct and another primitive superstition. Chief Eagle, you deal with the world on the terms demanded by the twentieth century, and it is obvious that you do not feel embarrassment practicing traditional Medicine, nor do you regard yourself as a superstitious person.

I agree with your point. If I am superstitious, one would have to call Abraham, Moses, and Isaac superstitious. They all went on vision quests; so did Jesus. They all went into the wilderness to fast. Moses received the Ten Commandments on a vision quest. The Bible may not use that term, but the biblical figures and the Indians practice the same procedure for the same purpose.

Do many Amerindians still embark on the vision quest?

Yes, there are quite a few people going on vision quests in the spring and the fall. On my reservation alone, there were six of them out at one time.

There are different levels of vision quests. Sometimes you can just go for a walk and meditate so that you can get close to nature. There is a strength in tranquility and peace. They provide energy.

If one wishes to go on the full vision quest, complete with fasting and the seeking of a guide and a vision, he walks in the footsteps of the saints throughout history who have communicated with God, the Great Spirit. The biblical figures did it; the Indians do it.

Again, I suppose, some might raise the criticism that modern man should emulate neither the spiritual practices of the prophets of two thousand years ago nor the life-style of "untutored savages" of several hundred years ago. How would you answer such a charge?

One time I gave a lecture in Omaha on the Indian religion. During the question and answer period, an anthropologist asked me, "How can you say such glowing things about the native American religion? How can you say that they were not savages? Isn't it true that some tribes practiced human sacrifice?"

I answered, "You have to examine the reasons why these tribes offered a human life in sacrifice. I have researched this practice among the Indians in Mexico, and I will admit that there were four tribes in the United States which practiced human sacrifice. In fact, there was one of them as near to us as Kansas, where they offered a pure person—and it wasn't always a virgin maiden, either. Why did they do this? There were three basic reasons: 1. So that they could retain their way of life; 2. so that they would have successful crops and prosperity; 3. so that enemy tribes would not war on them.

"Savagery or barbarism is really a relative term when one examines history from its beginnings. How do we retain such elements today in our dominant society? We put thousands of young men in uniform and have them slaughtered, desecrated, so that we can retain our way of life, so that we will maintain economic stability and prosperity, so that enemy nations will not war on us. I ask you, who is really the greater savage?"

The anthropologist sat down very quietly. The rest of the audience was applauding.

That is a very good parallel. Chief Eagle, what is your opinion of the Native American Church?

It has its rightful place, but I do feel it is misnamed. A "native American" church should emphasize traditionalism and traditional principles. I feel there is too much infringement of Christianity in their church. I feel a proper title would be the Native American Christian Church.

What is your opinion of Wovoka, the Peace Messiah, and the Ghost Dance?

I don't think Wovoka was a trickster. I think he knew himself that he was not a messiah. I think that was a label conjured up by other people. He had a prophetic message for people. I think we should all take another look at what Wovoka was teaching. The press and the federal system corrupted what he was saying, what he was trying to do for the

Indian people. Let us look at what he said, rather than at what happened after his words were corrupted.

Sitting Bull and the Sioux are usually given the discredit for that particular corruption. It was said that Sitting Bull was looking for a method of rousing his people to rebellion and seized upon the magic of the Ghost Dance.

I really can't agree with that theory. I think the Sioux agreed that Wovoka had a real message of peace. Wovoka's dance was supposed to bring down what the Christians would name the "grace of God." It was the white press and the white settlers' fear that transformed the ritual into a savage war dance.

Is there a place in the Lakota theology for such a concept as reincarnation?

Reincarnation is something that not too many Indians talk about.

Do you have a feeling of having been reborn? Do you feel you might have had an earlier life as an Amerindian before your present one?

Some of the elders have told me that although no one knows what Crazy Horse looked like, they feel that if I had been living in those days, I would have been just like Crazy Horse. But they tell me in this life, at least, I have a chance to live a long time!

I find Crazy Horse one of the most fascinating figures in American history. He was a solitary person who always followed his own Medicine. If he had been born a whiteman, he would have been regarded as an eccentric, perhaps a fool. Among the tolerant Sioux, there is provision for someone following his own Medicine, so Crazy Horse could become a great leader, a warrior-mystic. I know that even today he is regarded as a great figure among the Indian people.

He certainly is. You know, although he finally did surrender to the U.S. government, he never did sign a treaty, because he did not trust the System.

As soon as he surrendered, he was asked to go with his men up to the north country to help defeat Chief Joseph of the Nez Perce. This saddened Crazy Horse, but he said that he would go. He first gave a speech that is one of the most moving that I have ever heard. It is even more inspiring than Chief Joseph's famous speech. I must properly translate Crazy Horse's speech, because it was a mistranslation of his words that got him killed.

An interpreter said that, within the speech, Crazy Horse said, "I will take my warriors to the north country, and I will fight until all the cavalrymen are dead." Crazy Horse had actually said words to the effect that if the Great Father, the President, willed it, he would take his warriors to the north and fight alongside the cavalrymen, so that the wars might be ended, that all killing would cease, that they might all live in peace.

When General Crookes, whom the Indians called General Crooked Three Stars, heard the faulty translation, he, or someone on his staff, gave orders to eliminate Crazy Horse.

But it was a red soldier who bayoneted Crazy Horse.

It was a whiteman, Brad. There were too many witnesses among the Sioux prisoners who could testify to that truth. Crazy Horse died in his father's arms. His father's name was Wound.

Is it true that no one knows where Crazy Horse is buried?

That is true. Indian mystics have told me that I could find

exactly where he is buried. Some people know the area, but they say I can find the exact spot.

Would you ever do this?

What good would it do? The System would just want to dig him up so that they might examine the remains and find out what he looked like.

Why are the Black Hills considered sacred to the Lakota?

Because before the Great Invasion, everything the Indians desired could be found in the Black Hills. They believed that the Black Hills was the very heart throb of the Earth Mother. I think my book *Winter Count* tells you the feelings of the Indians about the Black Hills.

What would you say was the essence of the Lakota world view?

Humanhood. Treating your fellow man as a brother. Indians believe that all men are related and that we are only passing through this life as an exercise in dealing with our fellow man. How one treats his fellow man is a determining factor in how he elevates his inner spirit.

10

the legend of
the white buffalo

Every student of Amerindian culture has heard references to the legend of the White Buffalo. Occasionally, novels and motion pictures of frontier life will include scenes depicting the native peoples' "superstitious awe" of the sacred white buffalo. Here, for the first time, Dallas Chief Eagle has translated and shared the actual legend as it was set forth in the oral tradition of the Lakota people. The words are both powerful and beautiful in their simplicity, but do not be blocked from absorbing the universal and timeless relevance of the legend's message by the protective shield of pseudo-sophistication which modern man is supposed to have at the ready whenever he is exposed to "primitive myths." This legend has been repeated to countless generations as a teaching device. Do not be afraid to learn from wise ones who have long ago made their journey to the Spirit World.

My relation, I am an old man now, and I have seen many seasons file by like an animal procession to a water pond. Hear my tongue, my brother, for I have chosen this last sunset to tell you of an ancient legend. I feel the dawn will not follow the twilight of my life. When I sleep I will awake in the beyond, where there is no darkness.

This sacred legend had its beginning many winters before the Great Invasion from the dawn country. To ensure its continuation this legend is always handed down by men whose minds and eyes are wise and kind, men acquainted with sacred chants and meditations. This is why its exactness has never vanished. Being the present bearer, I hand down to you the "Legend of the White Buffalo." I hope your mind is ready to bind it for the next generation.

In an age before we had horses, in a season of budding spring, two braves went out scouting for the buffalo. For three days they hunted and tracked over plain, hill, and valley. On the fourth day, following the sunrise, the braves caught sight of a buffalo herd in a valley on the eastern stretch of the mountains. The herd was scattered across the valley.

The two hunters rushed their descent into the valley, and through habit of many hunts, slowed their pace as they neared the buffalo. Then it was, with equal surprise and joy, they noticed the white buffalo in the center of the herd. White with fur like winter etching, the prairie monarch stood motionless, enveloped in mystic vapor.

The hunters paused to robe themselves in wolf and coyote hides to kill their human odor, and readied their weapons. The buffalo throughout the valley began to move toward the White Buffalo, forming a circle around the White One. The two hunters moved cautiously toward an opening on the eastern side of the circle.

The music of nature does not fly in discord, and it was all around the valley. As the hunters crept closer to the opening in the herd, the spirit of the White Buffalo fully enveloped them, causing them to forget their desire to kill.

When the crouching hunters reached the opening, a blinding white flash brought them up straight. In place of the White Buffalo stood a beautiful woman in complete whiteness. In sunlight grandeur, she stood with hands extended, and the soft whisper of the wind made her hair, white skin, white robe, and white buckskin dress shimmer radiantly. Her mouth moved, and her voice, gentle and warm, flowed with a depth of sympathy that brought quiet to the valley.

I was here before the rains and the violent sea.
I was here before the snows and the hail.
I was here before the mountains and the winds.
I am the spirit of Nature.

I am in the light that fills the earth, and in the darkness of nighttime.
I give color to nature, for I am in nature's growth and fruits.
I am again in nature where themes of mystic wisdom are found.
I am in your chants and laughters.
I am in the tears that flow from sorrow.
I am in the bright joyous eyes of the children.

I am in the substance that gives unity, completeness, and oneness.

I am in the mountains as a conscious symbol to all mankind when earth's face is being scarred with spiritual undone.

I am in you when you walk the simple path of the redman.

I am in you when you show love of humankind, for I also give love to those who are loving.

I am in the response of love among all humans, for this is a path that will find the blessing and fulfillment of the Great Spirit.

I must leave you now to appear in another age, but I leave you with the redman's path.

Complete stillness was everywhere. The White Buffalo Spirit withdrew her hands, and with a glowing smile of eternal love, her body began to return to vapor.

One hunter could no longer contain himself from the beauty of the White Buffalo Spirit. His mind filled with extreme desire. He flung his weapons aside, brushed off his robe, and rushed for the fading spirit. A blinding flash again filled the circle. The White Buffalo Spirit was gone; the White Buffalo was gone; and all that remained was the skull of the charging hunter, gray ashes, and his formless bones.

This, my brother, is why we hold the White Buffalo to be sacred. The White Buffalo moves without the threat of an arrow or lance, whether we sight him in the northern forest, the plains country, or in the mountain regions.

I hope that your tongue can interpret the deep wisdom of this holy legend, and that you, my brother, may help to bring its message to all mankind.

11

indianism

DALLAS CHIEF EAGLE: It is incumbent upon the System to take a closer look at the American Indian and what he has yet to offer. We are talking about a potential food crisis. Why, for some strange reason, did the exploration of the Amerindian foods and medicines stop some eighty-five years ago? The whiteman is only toying with the surface of the knowledge that the Indian has.

You can go out on these prairies and see the Indian turnip. This vegetable will grow anywhere except where there is too much sand and gravel. It takes only the very minimum of water. It is high in natural phosphates. It has the same calcium content as corn. Look what corn has done for the world. This Indian turnip is just as valuable.

The American Indian still has many foods left to give to the System, together with special ways of cultivating them. With the ingenuity of the whiteman and the knowledge of the redman, there are many foods left to be given to the world.

And the System worries about birth control! Indians have always practiced natural birth control that has never required abstention from sex. Stop to think about it. The Teton Sioux, for instance, were nomads, always on the move. They couldn't afford to have big families, could they? Most couples had only one child. Three children would have been considered a very large family.

How did the Indians control their family size? There is a plant—a weed, if you will—that grows in dry areas. No, I do not know an English word for it, but a lot of it grows in the Badlands. The Indians went by the Moon—which would probably surprise the educational system. They had thirteen moons a year, a little over twenty-eight days per moon. Actually, the days of a year are a lot closer to thirteen moons than twelve months. Anyway, they took this tea by the moon. They drank it only once, and it kept them sterile for an entire moon. Either the man or the woman took the tea.

Then there is another birth control tea that is really quite phenomenal. Just the woman takes this kind. It is permanent. The woman cannot have any more children. In seven to eleven days, the tea atrophies the ovaries and eliminates the monthly period. In a week to a week and a half, the woman goes through her change of life. Instant menopause—with no aftereffects! And there are some white women who go through this change of life for several years.

I have an aunt who took this tea after having one child. It is terrific, harmless to the woman, and very effective. I think the American Medical Association is about one hundred years behind the American Indian.

I have heard rumors of such birth control methods, and they are truly remarkable. You know, Chief Eagle, I have often pondered on just how the ancient Medicine doctors knew which bark, which weed, which animal gland to boil, dry, grind, and serve. We know for instance, that the Indians boiled a certain bark that contains the same ingredients as our modern aspirin. The list of native remedies and medicines that have proven to contain the same chemical ingredients as the nostrums our most up-to-date laboratories can devise is really extremely long. What led those ancient herbalists to the right plants? It could not all have been just trial and error. I am certain the Indians of old took no more kindly to being poisoned than does modern man.

They were given the plants during vision quests. They learned of these things with the help of a higher power. Even now your researchers are finally learning that plants can communicate. Indians know of places where one can sharpen his senses. I feel that the next dimension is helping us in such matters. That is why the Indians will not tell the white people about some of these things. The Indian is afraid that the whiteman will abuse this knowledge, instead of considering it from a religious point of view.

The interesting thing about this birth control plant [he paused, took a specimen from his brief case] is that horses will not eat it. Cows, goats, buffaloes will not eat it. We have watched. In our theology, the Great Spirit creates everything for a purpose. If animals will not eat it, the Great Spirit has created it for a very special reason. In this case, it is natural birth control for the Indian. I am bringing this potion to a young couple who cannot afford to have more children. We do not want her to ingest chemicals for twenty years and risk harming her body.

Chief Eagle, to change the subject somewhat, I know that you are vitally interested in bringing more tourists to the area. Could you tell us about your philosophy as Director of Tourism for the United Sioux Tribes of South Dakota?

I am urging elaborate, educational package tours. We are fifteen years behind Europe in this area. Because of the energy crisis, the package tour will become increasingly valuable. In the package tour, we will be handling multiple people and families, not simply individuals. This will help alleviate fuel consumption. You can't keep people home, and they will travel the way they can save the most money. Package tours will the big thing starting this next spring. And we want to get some of that tourist money invested in the American Indian.

Might you expect to find some of your people fighting you a bit on this? Might some of them consider the prospect of dancing for tourists and having people gawk at them a bit demeaning?

Yes, and I recognize this grievance; but the point is, people are going to be coming anyway. I think tourism can really become the economic salvation of the American Indian. It all depends on how it is programed.

The tourist season lasts three months in this area. Why not extend it? Why can we not get into the audio-visual aspect of tourism? Why can't we Indians begin making our own movies? There are calendars to be produced, children's magazines, documentary filmstrips. There are so many things Indians themselves can do, providing they have the capital. This is where the government could give the Indians a big hand.

Along about here arises the export-import aspect of tourism. The market for Indian arts and crafts is not in the United States. The present market is in Europe and Japan. You would be surprised at how much they want this authentic stuff in Japan.

In January 1974, I will be giving lectures and displaying my paintings in Japan. I will also be meeting with Japanese investors. I think that if we cannot shake the money tree in this country, we might as well reach out and get foreign investments. Japan has a lot of people who eat a lot of food, and they do not have much food. We Indians would help them.

To get back to the complaint about tourists gawking at the Indians. Well, no one likes to be gawked at. But we can organize tourism in a sophisticated way.

Here is another point: The federal government grabbed ninety million acres of land from us Sioux and dumped us on useless lands with the command that we become agriculturalists. What is useless land for farming has since become priceless land for parks and recreation. We Indians are sitting on this land, and we have a wonderful opportunity to gain huge economic benefits.

At the same time, of course, you would also have a wonderful opportunity to teach both American and foreign tourists many of the basic truths of Indianism. Which brings a question to mind: Do you believe that Indianism can be taught?

Definitely. And, as an Indian, it hurts me that right now our colleges and universities are not teaching courses in Indianology. We have all kind of "ology" subjects in our educational institutions. We are identified throughout the world because of the American Indians. But yet, among all those "ology" subjects, we don't have a single course in Indianology.

I feel that Americans should investigate this area and learn the value of what the Indians have contributed to their cultures. I think the Indian value system could help Americans get along better in world crises.

When I was in Asia, I was told that the only people who have the solution to such struggles as Vietnam and the larger issues of world peace are the American Indians. Why? Because of his value system, his metaphysical culture, his philosophy. The Asians told me that the American Indian has a message for the world. But, I was also told, the Asians fear that the Anglos will never let the Indian truly project these values to the world.

That is a beautiful tribute that the Asians gave you as a representative of the Amerindian people. Could you state specifically to which Amerindian values they were referring?

I think you will find it throughout the pages of *Winter Count*. And you will surely find it in the legend of the White Buffalo, which I have shared with you. To my knowledge, this is the first time that the legend has been translated and actually put down in English. I think it has a tremendous message.

Let us say that we include courses in Indianology in our educational institutions. Would you, as a redman, feel any offense if I as a whiteman, together with my black friend, my yellow friend, take such courses? If we were to develop the proper attitude, could we become Indians?

Indianism is really a philosophy, an attitude, a way of life, which I think needs to be shared with people. I am quite proud of the men and women who wish to come to our way of life.

The following is an excerpt entitled "Indianism," which is taken from a paper that Chief Eagle prepared for the Plains Indians, urging increased involvement in organized tourism:

Indianism is our future. There is an ancient Indian saying that all plant and organic life go through a repeating four-stage cycle—infancy, puberty, adulthood, and old age (which is the reason Indians consider the number four so sacred). This same cycle is historically true of all human life. Nations and civilizations go through this particular cycle and eventually pass out of existence.

This is not a condemning approach to Indianism, but only a way to measure where we are today. We are at the last throes of a four-stage cycle. We have been in this stage for ninety years, resisting admirably the ignorant and subtle attempts to make us into non-Indians. Our Indian spirit has not been smothered, because our human constitution is made up of stronger moral fiber. Most of us still maintain our ethnic character and distinct cultural values; and despite pressures of all making, we have remained intact in direct challenge to the world values that are now being questioned.

To maintain Indianism with its human substance, we must evolve from the fourth stage crisis into a higher plane cycle of Indian development. This is the only avenue of pursuit that can guarantee us the perpetuation of Indianism. If you are proud of your Indian heritage and culture, then you must also be proud enough to care. Care enough to want to pay the price that the solutions demand. Care enough to make the effort, and to sustain the dedication. With this type of Indian concern and Indian input, we can methodically find solutions by breaking our problems down into components, so we can attack each area of the problems.

Self-determination means work! It also means that it will be left up to us Indians to make final determinations on what types and varieties of economic, social, and educational paths we will travel. This is the first time in nearly five hundred years that the System has given us the opportunity to promote the right of self-determination. Opportunity always provides one more goal!

Work is the key to self-determination, and even though it is the nature of man never to gossip about virtue, there are many Indians who are hard-working and keenly capable of being their brother's keeper. There are trails of pursuit opening up where we no longer have to submit to the seductive overtures of a confusing change. Now we can develop a bicultural existence that would assure us of our Indian life-style. It will mean putting the Indian stamp of our unique personality on the work we do. It will mean pouring our Indian spirit into the task. It will mean making our work representative of our faith in Indianism. It is only through work that leads to economic independence that we can retain our identity. We now have the opportunity to be the masters of our destiny.

The System has been commanding integration to us, but the logic of geography circumvents this intermingling. Now we will be able to choose and fashion the type of industry we need, so that dependency will no longer be part of our tradition. Through the exercise of traditional Indian minds and action, we will be able to lift ourselves out of the crisis of poverty and help the non-Indian world with their crises of war, racial conflict, and pollution.

Indians are not a contradiction to society. We have not been still for the past generation; we have forced awareness on the System; we have made the System bend. As a result, the Bureau of Indian Affairs structure has learned that Indians who know most about the imposed Indian problems are those who have the problems and who live with them, and that we can plan effectively when they give us the backing in our planning processes. The Bureau of Indian Affairs is an instrument for the Indians.

In essence, the new system calls upon us Indians to act as one nation (what our father's fathers had a hundred years ago). In other words, we are seeking to decentralize the Bureau of Indian Affairs, so that the detailed administration will be a local affair and lend itself to local Indian input. With this kind of involvement, a task can be done with high Indian standards in order to pave the way for bigger things. National equity, but local control.

The tourism industry is one of the most important branches of economic development in the United States and will continue to be for coming decades.

Region Eight is the land of the Indians. The Indians left an indelible stamp on this region. Evidence of that impression dots the area's terrain.

Indian tourism is investing in our future. For purposes of equity, Indian tourist development will be mainly on the Indian reservations in Region Eight.

The main assets of these Indian areas are: first, basically, the untouched natural beauty of Mother Earth. Second, to afford the tourist the opportunity to witness the original Americans in their home country, performing the dances and ceremonies that they know so well.

The process of exposing Indian cultural arts to the world will create employment. There will be need for lodging, food facilities; genuine Indian trading posts; driver-guides to operate small tour buses; salespeople to organize and monitor the sales of arts and crafts; trained professionals to create Indian export and import markets and the development of Indian audio-visual concepts.

The new front of the National Bicentennial Commission designation demands that "Region Eight needs Indians," and world interests demand that Region Eight develop a comprehensive tourist plan.

It is obvious that the best way to proceed in attaining our objectives is to improve a proper balance of relations throughout the whole region. Such a balance will require Indian input in all state agencies, organizations, and committees. We must immediately prepare appropriate information and channel it to all quarters which may be instrumental in the shaping of a tourist industry system which will provide the most for our visiting guests.

12

sun bear:
"man must
walk in balance
on the earth mother"

The first time that Sun Bear and I met in person, Wabun, his wife, had to separate us.

The reason for the forceful disentanglement was not due to our inability to strike a harmonious relationship or our inability to communicate effectively with one another. To the contrary, from the moment I had entered his mobile home lodge outside of Reno and had been embraced as a brother, we had not stopped talking. It seemed as though we were compelled to share a lifetime of experiences, visions, and dreams with one another before the Sun could rise on a new day.

"Come on, Sun Bear"—Wabun attempted to growl around an indulgent smile—"Brad and Dave Graham have traveled nearly two thousand miles to talk with you. They're not going to vanish during the night. Why not get some sleep so you can talk all day tomorrow?"

Sun Bear laughed and placed Ikamoo, the cat he had been stroking with occasional complimentary appraisals ("Isn't he one magnificent cat?" "Isn't he a heavy dude?") on the floor.

"You see," he told us, "the woman does not just keep to the background among the Indians. She has always been allowed to voice her opinion concerning any matter. The Indian woman has always had equality. That is why the whiteman fabricated this tale about the terrible slavery of the 'squaw.' He didn't want his own women to find out about women's lib any sooner."

Sun Bear scooped up two sleeping bags from a storage area off the kitchen. "Here, brothers"—he smiled—"we will treat you like tribesmen. No fancy beds."

Dave and I answered that we would consider such treatment to be an honor. Sun Bear and Wabun waved their good nights. Richard and Helen had turned in long ago. Ronnie, an attractive young Chippewa, had taken her bedroll to the Volkswagen bus next to the lodge.

There was a mattress on the floor or a couch against a wall. Since Dave has four inches on my own six feet, I volunteered to curl up on the couch. From the inquiring look in Ikamoo's eye, we knew that the cat would probably take turns sleeping with both of us.

I don't really think I slept at all that night. Sun Bear's soft, earnest voice and his recounting of ancient Chippewa prophecies and his own visions were very much with me.

Sun Bear seemed to generate a vortex of power, and the heavy Medicine vibrations of the Bear Tribe's encampment had suffused me with a kind of energy that made it very difficult to lie down and turn everything off until the daylight hours. I tried concentrating on the strong wind that sang a power chant of its own, as it rose and dipped in octave and volume, promising snow and cold and urging the completion of any winter preparations. But even listening to the wind-song, a sleep-fetching device I had employed with some degree of success ever since I was a boy, failed to lullaby me into anything more than a state of physical relaxation and a sense of well-being. My body rested, but my brain was actively framing dozens of questions for Sun Bear to answer.

Then time became a blur, and Sun Bear was once again before me, slouched in an old easy chair, legs crossed, a cup of tea cradled in his large, work-worn hands.

"We'll talk off and on between my work," he said. "There is much to do."

I nodded over the rim of my cup. Wabun had told us to come and stay as long as we liked, but that work for the Bear Tribe would have to continue as if there were no guests in the camp. One cannot expect more from busy people.

"We got a lot of walnuts yesterday when we came back from the craft show," Sun Bear said. His boots were still caked with mud. He seemed to notice my observation, and he laughed when he told me that the walnut grove had been so muddy that Wabun had come out of her shoes and he had let her get her stockings good and wet and muddy before he had carried her to dry ground.

"Many people let us pick up what they consider leftovers," Sun Bear explained. "We are not too proud to take them.

With the heavy times coming down, soon everyone will have to learn to become a good forager."

Sun Bear placed a sack of walnuts between his knees, grabbed a paring knife. "I will remove the covering from the walnuts, and you ask me questions."

He squeezed the rotting pulp from the nut, laughed as the dark stain covered his fingers. "Hey, I can rub this juice on me and become as dark as an Indian!"

Do some people come to you and expect to see you walking around in white buckskins with a pious expression on your face?

Oh, yes, quite often. I think they leave in disappointment because I don't bring out my rattle and shake it for them. They want me to give with some mumbo-jumbo to make me seem more real to them.

Your point is that Medicine is all of you.

Yes.

I asked Sun Bear to tell me about his childhood. "Come on, Sun Bear," I coaxed. "Let's do a 'This Is Your Life' bit."

He smiled, sat in reflective silence for a few moments, then reached for a fresh sack of walnuts to husk.

SUN BEAR: I was born in northern Minnesota, and I was brought up on the White Earth Chippewa Reservation.

I was about six years old when I got my first sling shot, and maybe I was about seven years old when my brother Howard taught me how to trap weasel. We would set traps in the culverts on the way to school. By the time I was nine years old, I had my first .22 rifle. I learned to appreciate it on the basis of what it was. It was a tool like an ax or a hoe.

We lived and hunted pretty much off the land, and in a few years I had 16- and 20-gauge shotguns. We had a few head of cattle, and we cut some pulp and cord wood to make a living. When I got a bit older, I would make $400 a year trapping muskrats.

Sometimes when I was about sixteen, I would go out and work on the farms in North Dakota. We worked on pitching bundles. This was during the last of the threshing before the combines came in. Those German and Russian farmers out there in North Dakota are really good workers. We might start at four o'clock in the morning. We would hitch up our teams and haul in bundles for threshing. The old tractor was there, but the horses brought them in. We got about eighty-five cents an hour. It was hard work, but I enjoyed it.

My dad had sheep and cattle, so we used to put up hay. He also used to cut wood and sell it in the cities. We would work out in the potato fields to make money, too.

We kids went to a country school south of Lundby, Minnesota. There were both Indian and non-Indian kids there, and it wasn't any heavy trip whether you were Norwegian or not. I learned to appreciate a lot of those Scandinavian dishes. I think all of us kids grew up with respect for each other.

When I turned seventeen, I started to work in some of the towns around there. I went to Fargo, Grand Forks, other places. I worked in a cemetery, a bakery. I finally got a pretty good job working for a garment company out of Chicago selling factory-direct suits. We would go from one town to another, selling made-to-measure suits. This gave me a way of traveling around, and I enjoyed it.

In about 1950, a group of us Indian people formed the White Buffalo Council in Fargo. We wanted to have something we could do together and work on together. We would have meetings, powwows, get together to smoke the pipe and talk things out.

In 1953, I was involved with the Wichita Warriors Club, but prior to that time, I had a thing with the U.S. Government.

Many white people are under the impression that Indian people don't have to go into the Army, but the reservations were subject to the draft the same as anywhere else. They kept pushing me to go into the Army. I was in there about three months when they started talking about this Korean thing. I was willing to get my duty in, but I was not about to fight Koreans. The Koreans hadn't taken anything from me. We Indians don't feel we have any right to murder people in other countries.

After about three and a half months, I could see there was no way of reasoning with these people, so I split. I was at Camp Chaffee, Missouri. I had picked up some good pointers on how to handle military equipment. But, basically, this just isn't where we're at. Man can't accomplish anything in reality with that sort of equipment. The thing of it was, the federal government was trying to get us to do its thing.

After I had split, I spent the time visiting other Indian people. I ended up in Reno after I had been at Santa Rosa working at the apple harvest. I lived with the Pimas. I got a crafts center going. This was way back before the war on poverty was ever heard of. We were trying to bring together a group of people and keep them working.

I would work picking spuds and onions to keep my eating money coming in, then I would take home an extra bag of onions to the people on the reservation. That was the way the old-timers used to do it. They would share and distribute to everyone according to need.

I was doing the work I believed in when the FBI came around and picked me up for splitting from the U.S. Army. I was taken down to the state air force base and flown to Fort Oregon for my sentencing. I got a fifty-seven-page court-martial. It took them a whole day to go through the whole trip on me. Officers' wives and other people were packed in the courtroom to see the scene of it. The word was that I was some kind of Indian Robin Hood.

The Army threatened me with all sorts of things. First, they were trying to say that I was guilty of treason. Not only had I deserted the Army, but I had used my influence in talking against the military.

I got a lawyer who was sympathetic to me. He argued that the whole thing was not a question of my guilt, but that I was a man who had come from another society and that I was consistent with my way of life. It was not a question of guilt, he said, but a question of whether justice would be done. He said the U.S. Government had a long history of aggression against the American Indian and that those acts should be considered at this time.

I ended up court-martialed, but it turned out to be an indictment against the United States, because I quoted Sitting Bull and Crazy Horse, and other outstanding Indian leaders. The major who was arguing my case got things down to a year; and due to many of my people in Nevada writing letters and petitions, I got out in seven and one half months on a military probation thing.

I went back to Nevada to work with my Indians. We had been in the midst of completing homes and we were building workshops for arts and crafts shows. The Army finally decided that I was contributing more working with my people than I would have been vegetating in prison. Here is a poem I wrote during my war-protesting days:

TO WAR! TO WAR!

It's the same cry of 50 centuries or more—the cry of rearm to war, to war. Captains shout and bugles blare
While muskets blast and rockets flare.
First it was the Egyptian Pharaohs host, then mighty Sennacherib with an army of which he boasts;
But down tumbled their kingdom, and Babylon rose high over all;
Then the steel-bowed Mede and Persians brought about its fall.
Greece the cradle of Democracy rose to fame,
Then war between Athens and Sparta came. Now Roman warlords brought bloody history on at a pace
For with their legions they sought to establish a super race.
When out of the North rode the barbarian Hordes,
As the Huns and Turks cut the Roman cords.
Now came mighty Charlemagne upon the scene,
And all Europe was conquered to fulfill his dream.
They said peace at last when treaties of West Holpia were signed,
But peace comes not to heart or mind.
Trouble by day and sorrow by night,
When will men learn that swords seldom bring right?
To the West now shifts the historical scene;
Taxation without representation, revolt will fight the scheme.

Then armies are marching, as a great nation is broken in two.
Two different flags waving,
And uniforms are one of grey, the other blue.
Peace for a time again,
Although small wars are waged every day and always it's sorrow with which the people pay.
But Mars God of War looks down on it all
And says, I'll stir them to battle, make the mighty one fall.
Great ones prepare proudly, the small ones in fright.
By the millions they mass; their banners are many fold.
It seems all Hell's broken loose, and death untold,
For mortar, airplanes, fire, and poison gas
Bring death and destruction to every class.
This is a war to end all wars, the politicians now cry.
After this will be peace; men will not kill and die.
We'll league the nations together, keep peace by disarmament.
This role will be better. But scarce had the din of battle died,
And dictator Hitler was marching with Mussolini by his side.
Blood ran in Spain, as Franco overthrew Governmental power.
Maps changed from day to day, as leaders fled their guiding tower.
But the war was fought and won,
And the Dove of Peace saw a new rising sun.
Then in old friends, new enemies are found,
And the post-war plan of peace is declared out of bound.
How will it stop? Where will it end?

Who knows, for these are but plans for mortal men.
For it is war or peace,
  As small nations fight to keep their fleece.
War in Cyprus and the Philippines,
  War in Viet Nam, Korea, and elsewhere behind the scenes.
But Oh! we have the United Nations now; and man will
bring peace through it somehow.
But can selfish man bring peace to this world of unrest,
Or will he have just smaller wars at best?
So while the Devil fiddles the Nation's dance,
Prepare for the battle, let each soldier sharpen his lance.
And it's the same cry that went forth for 50 centuries or
more,
The cry of rearm to war, to war!

*Can you tell us about your years in Hollywood portraying
bloodthirsty savages and bandidos?*

I spent about seven years in front of the cameras playing
cowboys and Indians. I worked on the "Brave Eagle" series
for CBS. At least he was a noble savage. I was technical director on that series. I did some parts, mostly walking around
in the background carrying my bow and arrow.

"Brave Eagle" was backed by Roy Rogers Productions, and
I had been hired direct from the producer's office. I worked
when the cameras rolled, regardless.

One time a new assistant director fired me because I was
playing checkers when he thought I should be doing some
new chores he had just dreamed up. When I came to work
the next day, he asked why I had come back, since he had
fired me. I told him that things did not work that way. I was

a personal friend of Roy Rogers' horse, Trigger, and I worked whenever the cameras did.

Russ Scott, Roy Rogers' cousin, and I were two extras who worked all the time. The producers had invented this whole Indian chief trip, and they really needed a technical director.

They had first spent about $75,000 on a pilot film about Cochise. But then the producer's son, who was a Boy Scout, informed Daddy that Cochise was an Apache, who never wore one of those beautiful Sioux headdresses. That shot the pilot down the drain.

Mike North, who had the brainchild in the first place, decided that they needed a technical director. They decided to dump Cochise, because that had become a public name, anyway, and create their own chief. They decided it was time to find out about teepees.

I would read over the script, telling them what should be changed to make it more authentic. Then I would go out on the set and look around. There would be a six-foot drum from the Congo. There would be J.C. Penney Indian print blankets hanging over the teepee flaps. I got rid of most of this crap.

Once Brave Eagle, who was played by Keith Larson, was hiding one of his braves because he had stolen some horses from the Blackfeet. I told Paul Andres, the director, that I did not see the scene at all. He asked me what would be the real scene of it.

"Brave Eagle," I said, "would be having a dance in honor of his brave for his having gotten his tribe some new horses."

Andres told me that Brave Eagle was a property-minded Indian.

I said, "Yes, he is the property of CBS!"

Whenever the six writers who did the series would run out of steam, they would call me and say, "Hey, Sun Bear. Why don't you come and have dinner with us?" They would pump me, and I would lay some ideas on them. The next thing I knew, another script would be out.

Once they used my name for a character, Chief Sun Bear, and the story ended up illustrated in a Dell "Brave Eagle" comic book. I used to tease people that I was star of stage, screen, radio, and comic books.

"Brave Eagle" was an interesting thing, and I worked for them for about six months straight. Then I dropped out and came back to work for the Indian people. When I got things squared away again, I came back and went into the "Broken Arrow" television series, which had Michael Ansara playing good old Cochise.

I got out of series work after this, and I became a free-lance actor. I even got to where I was grabbing Chinese parts away from the Chinese. I played a Tibetan brother in *Marriage-go-Round*, because I looked more a Tibetan type than anyone they could come up with. In *The Ugly American*, I played the Chinese sergeant who rescues Marlon Brando when the mob at the airport is pounding his Cadillac to pieces.

But the thing I liked best about television and motion pictures was that they gave me free time to do the work with the Indian people that I really wanted to do. During the time that I was acting, I worked with Indian centers, and I helped the women's clubs hustle money so they could buy boxes of groceries for needy families.

As I traveled around the country and visited the Indian people, I saw that they were beaten down more on the social scale than any other people. They had little sense of their culture, their heritage. In 1953, many of the Indian groups were considered nothing but a cheap labor source for the surrounding farmers and orchard growers.

The older people had been pushed through the government schools, and they had no sense of identification with their Indian culture. When my dad went to school, he was beaten if he spoke Indian. Those government schools were set up to divorce the Indian from his culture and to reward those who demonstrated by their attitude that they had turned their backs on Indian ways. If an Indian boy would run away from school and get caught, upon his return he would have to run a line of other Indian boys, lashing at him with military belts.

The whole philosophy of those Indian schools seemed to be: "Indian, you are not going to make out as well as a whiteman in this world, but we are going to make you over so that you can at least get some menial-task strips of it."

I feel that all labor is honest, and I see nothing wrong with working. But when society takes an entire race of people and conditions them to believe that they are fit only for manual labor and menial tasks, there is something very wrong with the System. If I went in cold to an employment agency, they would probably try to find a pick-and-shovel job for me. It makes no difference that I can write, that I can manage a television station.

Why have you chosen to live here, near Reno, Nevada?

This is an area where I can live near the city, make a livelihood with crafts and lecturing; and yet, if we ever have to get out of here, we can leave without having to be in competition with large masses of people fleeing the cities.

We are on the fringe of a city, but from here on the north, there is nothing but wide, open country. This puts us in a position where we can survive off the land.

You know, according to all the ancient Indian prophecies, we see us fast approaching the time of the Great Purification, so it will be important to be able to live off the land. This System is about to some crashing down.

When we traditional Indian people speak of the end of the whiteman, we are not speaking of a race, we are speaking of a way of life. A dog-eat-dog philosophy.

You know that my Medicine is for brothers and sisters of all races. Throughout the European's involvement with this land and its native peoples, many non-Indians have come to various tribes and have joined them. Even some of the early Jesuit fathers took off their robes and joined the Indians. They said, "Hey, these people have never read the Book, yet they have it going for them already."

I can sympathize and understand the work and Medicine and goals of a lot of the militant people, but their great feelings of hostility have grown to the point where they have no trust at all of any non-Indians. I cannot be a part of this, because I feel that we are moving toward a new society, a new way of life. If I were to copy this negative scene and perpetuate the idea of hatred toward another person on the basis of race, I would be imitating the thing I hate most—a rotten system of judgment that has been used to destroy people all over the world.

The black people in the cities have suffered from this and all the other crap that bigoted stupidity has put down on them. Now the turning point has come. They are going to declare a full vendetta on the System. If this happens, you won't be able to hold up your hand and say "I am your brother" because all that angry man will see is your face.

The people who really want to survive the destruction of the System and the Great Purification and who really want to live to find real brotherhood on the Earth Mother again will move away from these situations. That is part of the traditional Indian's warning: *Get away from the cities! Get out where there is safety!*

It is not a question of whether or not the Great Purification will be. It will. The whole of major cities will be destroyed. If one part of the prophecies is true, then all of the prophecies are true. The major confrontations in the Middle East are part of the plan. The Earth Mother is about to declare her complete rebellion.

The real thing of brothers and sisters coming together is to get to know one another and to get rid of all those old fears and phobias. That is what we have found.

Medicine is a part of me, and it does not have to be put off in a separate box. I tell people of the Bear Tribe how we raise crops, dry fruit, put up our stores. Some say, "We are more interested in learning Medicine. We want to go up on the mountaintop." All others want to know is where the peyote buds are kept.

First, you have to show respect for the Earth Mother. The making of love, the showing of love for the plants and fruits —these things are all part of Medicine. You don't separate Medicine from living. That is why the majority of the people in the System, the society that came to this country from across the Great Waters, have never had a religion that has been real to them. They do not take their religion beyond the church building. They never really taste their religion.

When I make a prayer, when I make Medicine, I do not do it only at a certain time. I do it when it is needed. Too many white people in the System are always bugging the Lord.

I have been to the meetings in churches, and I have heard them praying for television sets, for refrigerators, for new cars. I can see their picture: God is sitting up there answering all these telephone lines, sending out all the goodies. The way I have the picture, he is bursting with laughter and shaking his head.

Sometimes it is hard to be patient with those who say they want to go to the mountaintop when it is easy to see that they have not worked out a balance here because they are caught up in their own frustrations. Sometimes I tell them, "How can you go to the mountaintop when you can't solve your emotional problems? You are walking around with a hard-on and you haven't got to where you can relate to other human beings."

It is hard to have a relationship with God if you can't function on the level where you recognize that you are each others' brothers and sisters.

Those who seek a higher understanding of things must first lay a solid foundation and establish a good balance. On the basis of my experience and the experiences of my people, when you go up to make Medicine and fast to seek a vision, you are on the level of the Spirit World. If you are held back by all the worries of paying the rent and getting a new car, your mind just won't reach out.

Do you ever feel that you have done all this before?

Sometimes I have a sense of continuity. Sometimes I will be sitting down, and I see a lot of people that I have seen before. Lots of times I see them on the street. Many brothers, like Dave Graham here, I feel I have seen before.

Does such a concept as reincarnation fit in with Medicine Power?

I don't necessarily see this in the words of reincarnation. Too often reincarnation becomes an ego thing.

I see myself and other people as continuing forces in different forms.

Then there is the fact that we are all part of a whole. We traditional people are striving to bring this concept out—this sense of being part of a whole and sharing together a sense of responsibility on that basis. We are trying to reach out and put our hands on the shoulders of our brothers and sisters and say that we are all part of the same action.

13

the
bear tribe

Sun Bear founded the Bear Tribe in response to the ancient prophecies which foretold of a time when refugees from white society would come to the redman as lost brothers. Sun Bear is very survival-oriented, and he is firm in his belief that man can best survive by learning to develop harmony with the Earth Mother. The principles of the Bear Tribe, which apply to both Indian and non-Indian members, emphasize returning to the land and to the traditional Amerindian way of life.

At this time, Sun Bear wishes the site of the Bear Tribe near Reno to be the hub of a network of communes, rather than the actual physical home of all those who may desire to join the first new tribe of this century. The quarterly publication *Many Smokes* can thereby be a journal of communication for all those men and women who are seeking a tribal alternative to the economics of America.*

SUN BEAR: When people come to join our Bear Tribe, nobody speaks for another person. Each man and each woman has to speak for himself. No one can come to me and say he is speaking for his wife. Each person has to make his own decision. The Medicine that we see is people coming together as groups and becoming big families or tribes, living together in harmony.

The main things are loyalty, love, and sharing. If we have this Medicine in us, then the rest of it is no problem at all. The raising of garden vegetables and food is no problem if we have loyalty, love, and sharing.

We have to clean out the heads of people so that they can live together as human beings. We have to get rid of all the sicknesses, all the barriers that have been put in peoples' heads that have kept them separated. The worst thing about the System is that it separates people. We have been pitted against each other for survival for so long.

In the Bear Tribe, everyone must work. Medicine has to start with the raising of corn and plants. If your Medicine doesn't work there and you don't have things to feed your people regularly, then you really don't have any Medicine at all.

Indian religion was never a segregated kind of thing. It is a way of life. The reality of life is that everything is one con-

* As galleys were being read, Wabun wrote that the Bear Tribe had acquired land in Oregon that more totally fulfilled their needs. Those seeking information concerning the Bear Tribe and the journal *Many Smokes* should direct their correspondence to Post Office Box 1961, Klamath Falls, Oregon 97601.

tinuous stream of Medicine. We are finding that the growing of crops and food is the first thing to accomplish. If you can't find the balance in raising crops, you won't find it going to the mountaintop.

The System has bred a real sickness where it has gotten people harnessed into paying their little $20,000 mortgages on their little houses and their little cars. It has tricked them into trying to survive on that stupid basis instead of raising their own vegetables. Our Medicine is strongest when we can break people of having to run to the supermarket for every crumb of food and have someone put the twist on them for more dollars. I feel happy for everyone I have liberated from the supermarkets and taught how to go out and gather acorns and harvest them.

Two or three years ago, when I was preaching about an energy crisis coming, about rationing gas and things, people said I was just a prophet of doom. Now they have to look hard at what I am saying, because there seems to be some truth in it. They are now going to have to get out their wood stoves to keep warm. They can't look toward that Great White Father System to supply them with everything they need any more.

Ultimately, we see the time when humanity will walk on the Earth Mother as one big family. There will be respect for one another. Right now, it could be a tight scene if we went up into the mountains without some rules.

The oath of our tribe pledges that we will not partake of liquor, hard drugs, or possessiveness. I respect the right of other people to use liquor and drugs, but I tell those who come here that we do not practice the usage of such things, and if they live here, they cannot use them either. I have seen little kids trampled at powwows. I have seen too much violence when people are drunk. We are reaching for a responsibility of love. Our Medicine is not a meeting on Sunday, and then everyone goes off and does his own thing. A person has to give, not just receive.

We do not have many people in the Bear Tribe at the present time. Not long ago, there were many, many more, but a bad thing happened.

I had gone to New York to tell people what we saw coming, the Great Purification, the cleansing of the Earth Mother. I had to tell them that I saw that people must come together and form groups and become self-reliant. People must go out on the land, but they must not come to the Earth Mother to perpetuate the same sicknesses, the same selfishness that they had in the System. They must learn to come there with better hearts and with a real sense of love and respect for each other. I had seen these things. It was my vision to tell people.

When I came back to the Bear Tribe, I saw that, for too many people, Medicine had only been a thing of the lip, not the heart. Before, we had harvested vegetables and dried fruit. We had harvested about four tons of crops that year. Now some of the men, whom I had taken into the tribe as brothers, were on different things than they should have been on. One of the brothers had been pressured to go back on the psychedelic drug trip.

I was heartsick. I couldn't eat. I told them again that these things were not my Medicine.

Finally, I went up on top of a mountain. I took off all my clothes, because your own body is the only thing that is really yours. The first thing I saw was an eagle circling around above me. Little clouds were scattered in the sky. A big cloud began moving over. I watched it. A little cloud came out from the big one. It was a very still day, but this cloud came out and began to spin like a whirlwind. After a while, just a little bit of the cloud went back to the big cloud. I had been told what would happen to the Bear Tribe.

I went back to the camp, and I said that those people who see and who take the same way as I did could come with me to Reno to begin a new camp. In Reno, there would only be the Bear Tribe and just our own Medicine. Those who wanted Timothy Leary's or someone else's trip should not come with us. We wanted only those with us who had a sense of work, love, and responsibility. We didn't want freeloaders and those who practiced psychedelic Medicine. It was sad, but only a few came with me.

Annie Bear, Nimemoshe [Loving Woman], you have been with the Bear Tribe for eight years. How did your association with Sun Bear begin?

ANNIE BEAR: I met Sun Bear when I was attending Berkeley. I dropped out of school with a week remaining before my graduation. Sun Bear and I have toughed out rough times together. I work with *Many Smokes,* stuffing mailings, doing artwork.

Why have you stayed with the Bear Tribe?

Obviously it has not been for the money. I have stayed on because this has been a personal accomplishment. It has developed my rules for the world. My background was limited to white, middle-class. When I learned that there was a broader view to the world, I wanted to participate. I feel that my involvement with the Bear Tribe has been a constructive way to be a part of meaningful things that are happening.

What is it that Sun Bear is doing that makes you feel that there is more here than working with some other group?

I am loyal to the tribe, but they are also loyal to me. We watch out for each other, and such a sense of loyalty barely exists in a society where everyone is so competitive.

How would you articulate the ideals of the tribe?

It is one of those things where people have a responsibility to teach others. Whoever comes to the tribe has quite a bit of adjustment to make, because most people have never seen anything like this before.

What was the biggest adjustment you had to make?

None of the adjustments were terribly bad for me, because they came gradually in my case. When I first met Sun Bear, the tribe didn't exist. This was something we built together with some of the other good people who joined in later.

SUN BEAR: Many people at that time were coming to me and wanting to join me, but I didn't really have anything for them to come and join. I didn't feel the need at that time to go through with what we are doing now. At that time, I tried to help people by telling them about living in harmony with brothers and sisters on the Earth Mother. A good relationship between brothers and sisters is so important, because if you can't accomplish this, you can't begin to reach higher.

ANNIE: The system in which I grew up had alienated me. It offers such a competitive trip that some people are left in the dust with no assurance that they are going to survive. The Bear Tribe is a group that is interested in survival, but we are not interested in enriching ourselves at our brothers' and sisters' expense.

Ronnie just asked if she could use my sewing machine. Well, it is not really my sewing machine. It is a piece of equipment that belongs to the tribe that happens to be in my custody. We've found that we do not need to be selfish and competitive. There is no need for it. I think we are going to be working on this shared feeling even more. Sharing works, and the System doesn't.

What about the spiritual aspects of the tribe. Are they meaningful to you?

Yes. We do our purification practices where we feel physically better. The very fact that we live on earth, instead of concrete, almost automatically enables us to pursue spiritual matters. The spiritual aspects of anything are, of course, very personal.

May I ask for your personal feelings in this regard?

I don't personally discipline myself a great deal in order to obtain a spiritual level. To breathe real air and to go out and see the earth and mountains makes me happier and certainly elevates me spiritually.

Do you find it possible to carry your Medicine back into the city?

I find it difficult to practice anything surrounded by dirt and noise and clutter and insanity. I grew up on a farm in Rhode Island, so it is hard for me to adjust to a city and to be happy there. It seems to me that whenever I run into people who are interested in spiritual matters, they are interested in leaving the cities.

What about those who might accuse you of being a hopeless romantic and suggest that since you couldn't make it in contemporary society, in the city where the action is, you are desperately clutching to some dream life?

If you are interested in surviving in the System, then what we have out here would be a dream. But we are not interested in surviving in the System.

You left Berkeley with one week to go. Was that a retreat on your part? Were you running away? Or was it a time to withdraw and get yourself together?

I was kind of running away from nothing. I was in school because Dad was paying for me to go there. I think that was the only reason I was there. And that was not much of a reason. The first time I found something that might happen, I wanted to pursue it a little further to see if it would. In Sun Bear and the Bear Tribe, I believe there is something that is more realistic, more lasting, than the System.

Dennis and Christine Poitras are a young couple from Massachusetts, both twenty-three years old. Together, they have a child, Justin, and hopes for the future. Dennis is an accomplished painter, a talented musician. Christine wants to be a good wife and mother, and she worries about the direction society has taken in recent years. I asked them why they had recently joined the Bear Tribe.

DENNIS: When Sun Bear lectured in Massachusetts, he gave us an invitation to drop by and see his people and see what was going on, so we stopped on our way to California. Here with the Bear Tribe has been the only place that seems like home. It is so warm and wonderful.

CHRISTINE: Everything that Sun Bear has going is much of what we want to do. The ways of survival. Learning the things of nature—how to use them and how to find them. There is not that much reason to do things when you are sitting in a fifth-floor apartment in the city. There is so much that these people have here and so much that they want to teach me. And I really want to learn. It just feels like the most natural thing to do.

And you have been with the Bear Tribe for only about two weeks. Is that correct?

DENNIS: Yes, about two weeks. But in the spirit, a long time.

CHRISTINE: We have been struggling so hard to survive for so long. We have tried so many ways. We have tried to do things honestly and by hard work. But we just couldn't keep up with things. We couldn't be comfortable and happy on what we earned. So we got a loan and paid some of our bills and bought a car and left.

DENNIS: When we arrived here, we had ten cents left in our pockets. We wanted to join Sun Bear in his vision and make things happen in a positive way.

[Wabun (Dawning Wind), Sun Bear's wife, was born Marlise James twenty-eight years ago in Newark, New Jersey. Although she has a trace of Indian blood on her father's side of the family, Wabun is white. She is a graduate of the Columbia School of Journalism, the author of *The People's Lawyers*.]

WABUN: I have been writing since I was seven, professionally since I was fifteen. I worked as editor and managing editor in several new youth magazines that went under during the recession. I started writing *The People's Lawyers* because I had been interested in becoming a lawyer myself, but I couldn't stand the thought of three more years of school. When I came out to California to interview lawyers and do research on the book, I was searching for a teacher, a teaching, something I could follow and to which I might become committed.

Had you been a member of a mainstream orthodox church?

I was a fanatic when I was a kid and a teen-ager. I was a Presbyterian, and I really thought that if I missed one Sunday going to church, I would go to hell. When I went to college, I began to miss a couple Sundays, and I noticed that I didn't feel any more sinful for it. The hypocrisy hit me and I began to taper off. Religion didn't seem to answer any questions that couldn't be answered in political terms.

I was a political person for a while. I was an active youth leader in several national associations and councils. I even went to Johnson's inaugural ball. I thought I would become a revolutionary, but although I have violence in my nature, I am not that violent.

A good friend of mine introduced me to the Gurdjieff philosophy. It hit me at the right time, and I did a lot of the reading for it. I was also interested in Sufism, and I had attended some Sufi meetings. By this time, my political nature had become over-ridden by metaphysical things.

When I was in California, I heard about the Bear Tribe, and it sounded interesting. Some people were voicing a lot of criticisms about the tribe; but to me, their criticisms seemed like valid reasons for being interested in Sun Bear and his work. I was invited to a big potluck the weekend I was out there, but I had too much to do on my book, so I didn't go.

I am glad, in a way, that I didn't go that day, because I might not be here now. I am somewhat wary of large groups and things that don't seem very disciplined. But I did think that Sun Bear would make a good magazine article. On the misinformation I had, I thought he was a seventy-year-old Hopi who tottered around in a blanket and carried a walking stick. My friend with the tribe kept me informed about their activities, and Sun Bear finally visited me in New York City. It was an immediate, very high thing between Sun Bear and me and the tribe.

I felt I couldn't leave New York, because I had a book to finish and that was where my commitment was. I went through several very bad months trying to decide between the work I was involved in and coming out here. Finally, I made up my mind to come out and see what was what.

I was not very constructive to the group for several months after I got out here. At the end of every week I was leaving —but I never did. Eventually it got around to me that maybe, for some reason, I was being led to see where I belonged. I took the oath to the tribe, and I tried to be as conscious of what I was doing as I could be. From the beginning, there has been a very strong personal attraction between Sun Bear and myself, which has strengthened. Sun Bear and I work well together. I really do believe in his vision now.

You believe, then, that the Great Purification will soon be upon us, that destruction has already been written in the Spirit World?

This might be difficult for some people to accept, even if they don't especially like the way the world is going now. To think of chaos and the cleansing of the Earth Mother to create new order is a heavy concept. It will be dirty and nasty, and we won't like it; and it is going to send a lot of people insane. If you really take it and accept it and see what is predicted, you know most of the people on the earth are going to die from the process of cleansing—your family, your friends, many will be taken. It is not an easy thing to think about. It took me a long time to get it down.

And you believe that the traditional people across the world have the responsibility of protecting the land and that they must get back to tribal life and traditions?

Yes. I believe further that when things are going through rapid changes, there is a lot of energy to be picked up, metaphysical energy, or whatever you want to call it. I also think that to keep developing, you have to stay alive. I think that things might really be a lot different after the Cleansing. If I am alive, surely, I have a lot better chance of getting it together in this lifetime than if I am dead. That's why I think what we are doing here in the Bear Tribe is so important. I think survival is good.

Do you ever get any static from redneck elements—both white and red—who might object to Sun Bear's vision of a tribe of mixed racial elements?

I found that when I was most conscious of being a white with an Indian, at powwows and craft shows and things, people would react more. Now, I feel more Indian than white, so people don't pick up on me. A lot of Indians who are full-blooded aren't going to agree with that.

Being Indian is, well, it is more than an attitude. It's . . .

Indians don't speak or talk nearly as much as white people do. The less you talk about emotional things, the less head-tripping you do and the better off you are. That is what kept me messed up when I came here. I was head-tripping all the time. I couldn't see anything around me.

To be Indian is a feeling more than an attitude. An attitude is a mental thing, something from the mind, not the heart. I think a lot of people who are half-Indian by blood aren't very Indian. They can be rednecks of the worst sort. People who are falling over each other drunk as hell have no better chance of making it through the cleansing of the earth because they happen to be browner than white people.

What is there about Sun Bear that really makes all this retribalization work?

You rarely meet people who truly have a direction in life. Most of us are flopping around all over the place. Most people are looking for a direction, but they can't commit themselves to real things. Sun Bear is committed to his vision. With Sun Bear, you get a feeling that he means what he is saying.

It is hard to make a commitment. I don't know how hard it was for the other people here, but it was hard for me. Real commitment is not something that is taught, or even condoned in this society. Committed people are fanatics—no matter what they are committed to. That is the societal point of view.

I feel that Sun Bear has given me a direction. I am happy here. I am a high-energy person, and there is always work to be done around here.

What do you think would be the hardest adjustment for someone to make who comes from the System into the tribal structure?

To eliminate competitiveness. Competitiveness is really bred into society. It is hard to be brought up anywhere in society—whether middle-class suburb or reservation—and not be competitive. In the tribal ideal, as I understand it and as I have experienced it, competition is not necessary. It takes a lot to get competitiveness out of someone who has come from structured society.

Where is your head now, Wabun?

I know that good Medicine is more a spiritual than a physical thing. I know that I would rather build than destroy.

I want to find a balance in myself, so that I can get to a point where I won't get thrown off balance by little things. Negative emotions are unnecessary. When I was political, I used to think that I could change the world. Now I believe if I change myself, I will change the world.

14

storing food for survival

Some of our prophets say that the white man came here because he had to learn a balance with nature from the Indians. They say that because the majority of them haven't learned, their world of lies is tumbling down. The wise men also say that the white man came here so that our people would see their own possessiveness and the divisions that kept Sioux and Chippewa apart, and caused our intertribal wars and sufferings. Look at the white society, then search your heart to see if you're correctly learning the lesson the whites were sent to teach.

If we are to be truly brothers and sisters on the land, we must walk with a good balance.*

Sun Bear

It is our belief that only those people living on the land in groups in harmony with each other and the Earth Mother

* From *Many Smokes*, Fall, 1973, used with permission.

will survive the coming cleansing of the Earth. And for these groups to survive, they must be prepared. That means that they must have stored enough supplies to sustain the group for a period of three or more years.

What will you need to survive? First of all, water. If you have chosen your land well, you will have a good natural water supply that will flow without interruption. A spring or well is the best alternative. If you get your water from a stream it might be cut off or become unsafe during certain periods of the cleansing of the Earth. To make sure you'll have some water if such periods arise you should fill some glass or plastic containers with fresh water, store in a safe place, and check every few months for leaks and freshness. Figure on a minimum of one-half gallon of water per person per day for drinking. To use water that is unsafe, purify it by boiling for one to three minutes, then pour it from one container to another several times to get some air and flavor back in. You may also purify it by adding any bleach that has hypochlorite as its only active ingredient (eight drops to a gallon of clear water, sixteen if the water is cloudy) letting the water sit for a half hour and checking that the chlorine smell is still there. If it isn't, add another dose of the bleach and let stand for another fifteen minutes. You may also use 3 per cent tincture of iodine. Add twelve drops to a gallon of clear water, and twice that to cloudy. Or you can use water purification tablets if you have them.

Next you should have on hand a large supply of any prescription medication needed by members of your group: birth control pills, heart pills, allergy pills, insulin, etc. Then, of course, you'll need food, seeds, canning and drying equipment, fishing and hunting gear. Having a varied diet is very essential to keeping your balance, so we really urge any of you who think you can live completely off the land to re-think your plan. While you can get your meat through hunt-ing, and forage for wild greens, berries, herbs, and fruits, we believe that more variety than that is necessary. If you have a good supply of seeds you can grow your own vegetables, then can or dry them for the fall, winter, and spring when you can't get them fresh. Besides canning equipment (re-member to have three or four times the number of lids as jars and rings) you'll need sugar or honey for canning fruits and jams, and vinegar, dill, and spices for pickling.

Because growing a garden may be difficult or impossible for a year or two we suggest that you have canned foods, and dried ones, on hand. For a family of five you'll need, on the average, two cans of soup per day, two of vegetables, one meat, and two fruit, plus five cans of juice per week. In addi-tion, for a year you'll need at least twelve three-pound cans of shortening, six cans of baking powder, and four gallons of Clorox for water purification.

Besides your fruits, juices, and vegetables you'll also need some staples. With a mixed diet an adult will use three hun-dred pounds of wheat per year, or one hundred pounds of flour. Wheat is cheaper to get and easier to store than flour. Make sure to get a hand-powered grinder with a stone burr to grind the wheat. Each adult will also need eighty pounds of powdered milk, one hundred fifty pounds of dried beans and peas (including soybeans, your best nonmeat source of protein), sixty pounds of sugar, fifty pounds of honey, and fifty pounds of peanut butter per year. In addition to the above, store any items that you're used to having in your diet: for instance, coffee, tea, herbs for tea, oats, rice, barley, nuts, hard candies, salt, pepper, spices, vinegar, oil, dessert mixes, corn meal, potatoes, syrup, molasses. To figure out how much you need to store, mark boxes or jars and see how much you use over a two-week period and figure that amount times twenty-six for a year's supply. Store things that will keep well and store them in moisture-, mouse-, and insect-proof containers wherever possible.

What hunting and fishing gear you'll need depends on what you are used to and can use. Unless you think you want to be a vegetarian (which we don't recommend, especially in a period of anarchy) you should know how to use something. A .22 is a good all-around gun, but you have to be a good shot to get small game with it. Shotguns are good for that. Get the right ammunition for the guns you have and get plenty of it. For fishing get plenty of line, an assortment of hooks, flies, sinkers, and a float. You can make your own pole, and, later, your own flies. In case you hit a period where no game is available to you, we suggest having a supply of jerky, dried fish, and canned meat and fish on hand.

You should also have in storage (or in use) tools that you are likely to need. These should include a good case skinning knife, a sharpening stone, a double-bit ax, a saw, shovel, hammer, screwdrivers, nails, screws, hoe, spade, pliers, pots, pans, plates, bowls, silverware, long-handled fork, matches, several canvas tarps or large pieces of heavy plastic, a fire grill, canteens, rope, washboard, pails. And you should stock up on sanitary and personal items: soaps of all kinds, disinfectants, cleaning solutions, toilet paper, sufficient bedding for everyone, personal clothes, sweaters, heavy jackets, and rain ponchos, sewing equipment, craft supplies, good hiking or woodsman boots, boots or overshoes for winter, work gloves, tooth equipment (include dental floss), sanitary napkins or Tampons, towels, extra underwear, alcohol, ammonia, aspirin, bandages, Band-Aids, cotton, ear drops, epsom salts, paregoric, safety pins, shampoo, thermometers, tweezers, antihistamine, liniment, calamine lotion, Vaseline, snake-bite kits, insect repellent, and vitamins. You'll probably also want reading and writing material, cards and other games.

You'll also need to store different fuels to combat the present fuel shortages, and the worse ones that we'll face in the future. Gasoline is a good fuel that can power not only your car but generators and various other things as well. It can be stored in the metal gasoline cans made specifically for that purpose, or in metal drums. For reasons of both safety and security it is probably best to bury the drums, and not let people see what you are doing. Unleaded gasoline can also be used to fuel Coleman stoves and lanterns. We don't feel that either natural or propane gas will be available for use for much longer, nor do we recommend storing them. Other than gasoline, the only other fuel we feel will be relevant is wood (or possibly coal if you're in an area where it is available). Wood is a good fuel for both heating and cooking, and it is easily available in most areas. We think that you'll be safe if you just have a year's supply ready in advance. In any case, you should always get in your winter's supply before it gets too wet and cold to do so. Four to eight cords of wood should be enough for the heating and cooking needs of a four-room cabin, depending on the area in which the cabin is located. For additional light needs you should have a good supply of candles, flashlights, batteries, kerosene lanterns, and, of course, kerosene.

We know that we've suggested storing a substantial

amount of goods of all kinds and that it will be costly to do so. However, we can't think of any safer investment you can make. While we are geared to having small groups together on the land, we feel that you should start storing these supplies wherever you are and whatever your family structure. But we do urge city dwellers to at least think of places in the country where they might be able to store some of their supplies. We think you should start gathering your storage supplies now. While we can't put a date on when we think the System will destroy itself completely, we don't think there is much time left. And it's better to have your survival supplies ready a year too early rather than an hour too late.

15

practicing
medicine power

Let us visualize the following scene: It is a pleasant autumn night. The leaves have turned from green to brilliant daubs of red and gold. The moon is full, and only a few clouds occasionally screen its light. The air is chill enough to make one appreciate a warm jacket or sweater and to encourage one to move closer to the campfire. Twylah has just poured herself another cup of coffee, and she holds the steaming pot over your own cup. Sun Bear is filling his pipe with *kinnikinick*, the native tobacco made of herbs. Dallas Chief Eagle is reaching for a fresh cigarette. The talk is about to turn to that of how one might best practice Medicine Power.

SUN BEAR: Medicine Power to our people means many things. Medicine is different herbs to be used in healing. There is the sweat lodge. There are various healing poultices.

It is when the Medicine man has the particular gift of knowledge that enables him to go into the Medicine lodge and talk to the spirits. All these things are Medicine.

My own thing is that I smoke a pipe and ask for Medicine. Sometimes I smoke it all the way through and ask for Medicine. Sometimes when energy forces are being used against me, I will smoke my pipe and hold them back.

Would you explain the Medicine coins you carry?

SUN BEAR: My Medicine coins were given to me as a gift by a bronco Apache. The bronco Apaches are brothers who travel back and forth across the line from Mexico and the United States. They have never eaten the bread of the whiteman. They don't depend on the Bureau of Indian Affairs or anyone else. They live entirely on their own resources. When they want food, they kill whatever is near—whiteman's cattle, deer, or donkey. They raise crops in the mountains. They have never come down and embraced this society.

These brothers, when they heard of my work, gave me these coins. See the dates? They range from 1832 to 1891. I am certain they would be of value to collectors, but their real value lies in the fact that they are Medicine coins. There are four of them. Four is a symbol of completeness to our society. Four is representative of Medicine itself.

One time a Flathead Indian I had befriended was left in charge of our place while I was gone. His loyalties were more to the firewater bottle than they were to the tribe. He couldn't really understand what we were doing in the Bear Tribe, even though we had taken him in and tried to help him. He stole my Medicine coins and took them with him to Montana. My brother, Sun Dancer, who is also a Flathead, went up there and brought them back. The man understood that he must return them when he learned the coins were Medicine.

What other Medicine items do you carry?

SUN BEAR: I have in my own Medicine bag a stone given to me by my sister Wabun. I have a meditation stone that comes from the Orient. Here is a shamrock that was given to me by one of the Irish who feels very strongly about his people. I have a piece of turquoise.

The Bear Tribe has a Medicine bundle with a pipe. There is a patch of cloth that has the blood of all our brothers and sisters on it. Whenever a person takes a blood oath to the Bear Tribe, his blood goes on that patch. Our bundle also has Medicine stones in it. The pipe is of catlinite and it has feathers and things that people have given it.

DALLAS CHIEF EAGLE: I have a rattle, a very special rattle. The Yuwipi people told me that if I should ever lose it, I would only have to go back to a certain place in South Dakota, and it would be there waiting for me. You will never see a rattle of this type in any museum. It is too sacred. One time I tried to get its beat on a tape, but it was impossible to record it. Whenever I go on any trips, I always carry my rattle with me.

What is the meaning of the pendant around your neck, Chief Eagle?

CHIEF EAGLE: It is the Indian star. The Star of David has six points; the Star of Bethlehem has five; and the Indian star has eight points. The colors of red, yellow, black, and white are sacred colors to the plains people, particularly the Cheyenne. There is no special Medicine significance to the pendant, however.

How do you use your dreams to give you direction?

187

SUN BEAR: I use my dreams in many ways. I use them as a sense of warning to advise my brothers and sisters against danger. I use dreams to give me ideas to develop later. I have even used my dreams in gambling.

I had a dream last night which I cannot yet discuss. It is about something that will be happening on some reservation. I may be involved as well. I need to re-evaluate the dream.

Some things that I see, I cannot always tell my people, because they are not yet ready. I know of certain shortcuts to get to where we have to go. In Medicine, some things are of value to yourself personally. Like some Medicine people have power chants which can be passed down and used by only one family.

TWYLAH: I follow very closely the goals which I have set for myself, so my personal symbols will not appear not only in my dreams, but in everything I do. One of my symbols is the circle. It is balance, equality, unity. To me, dreams are guidelines. And my dreams and visions come to me by day, as well as by night.

But I do not force things. I do not go to bed with a problem on my mind and think that it will be solved by morning. I do not feel that I can force the dream, but what I can do is to open myself and become receptive. My advice to anyone is to open up and let the thing come down to you.

Do you think that dreams that might come through a chemical stimulus would be as reliable as dreams that come naturally?

TWYLAH: I have never used anything of that sort, so I am not in a position to give feeling toward it. I cannot answer for anyone else. My opinion is that the dream or vision would not be as pure as that which came through a natural opening-up. I think that anything that would be forced would have its limitations.

What about the vision quest? How should one go about preparing himself to receive his Medicine?

DALLAS CHIEF EAGLE: First, I would tell the seeker to cleanse himself spiritually. Take a sweat bath. After this, don't touch any food. You may drink some water. Go somewhere where you will have a minimum of interference. Then, sitting, kneeling, or standing, meditate. Think on why you are there.

Between a day and a half to three days, I should say within four days, the message will come. The message may be received in English or in some other language, but you will understand it, the entire concept. Or you might receive the message in the form of a chant. In ancient times, Indians sang their prayers, because they felt singing was of a higher level than ordinary speech.

SUN BEAR: I did not go on my actual vision quest until I was in my twenties. Before the coming of my realization of what I must do with my life, I spent much time seeking my direction and learning from accomplished Medicine people. I spent time with the Hopis, the Navahos, and many other tribes. I learned from the Peyote brothers, and I gained respect for their Medicine. Since those days, Medicine has come to me at different times and in different ways.

One time I was on top of a mountain when I received a vision of an earthquake. The next day, I called a friend in Los Angeles, and things had happened as I had seen them in my vision.

In other visions, I have seen the destruction of the System. I have seen armies and bands roaming the cities. I have seen bands made up of former policemen gathering up their brothers and fighting to stay alive against bands made up of revolutionaries who gathered when they saw this nation, this System, being broken down by natural disasters. When the Great Cleansing comes, there will be many who will pick at the bones of the dying System.

What techniques do you employ to stop the world, to enter deep states of meditation?

DALLAS CHIEF EAGLE: I think the mind can be made to absorb itself and expand itself. I think one can do intense meditation, and I think one can cultivate this ability. I concentrate intensely on a subject. I assume no special body position. I take careful pains to guard against being disturbed. I've tried to meditate in forests and beside streams where there was too much interference. I must reach an area of complete solitude. If one gains a proper avenue for introspection, the mind absorbs itself—then explodes, bringing knowledge to the seeker.

I think this knowledge comes from a higher power. Sometimes when you speak in this area, you lose a lot when you use the term "God." You may lose proper perspective of a subject that has become so associated in our society with Christianity that God is considered only from that point of view.

I think there are levels of power and intelligence, and I believe you can reach a definite higher level of energy through meditation and intense concentration. I don't think it takes the mind long to grow accustomed to rising to higher levels and to learn how to gain proper knowledge from different levels of energy and power. I think it is quite possible to train the mind to reach these unknown dimensions.

TWYLAH: I can get off the world very easily. One of my devices is to put myself in a mental drain tile. I put spiritual protection around everyone, and then I place it around myself so there is complete balance. All the spiritual forces are opened up so they can circulate and everything goes in balance.

When one is in the process of learning, the material world can be so pronounced that the student leans in the direction of worldliness. The spiritual self does not come through because it is being shut off. In order for the spiritual light to function the way it should, the teacher has to do something drastic to make the student stop what he is doing wrong and get him back to the real thing—learning about himself and his environment.

I'll tell you how I used to meditate with my grandfather, Moses Shongo. In the morning we would sit on the porch and watch the Sun as it would come up. We would say thanks for the things for which we were grateful—things below the ground, on the ground, above the ground. In other words, we would progress from the material to the spiritual.

The moment you are born, you breathe in the breath of life, the most important gift of the material world; but prior to birth, you have been endowed with the spiritual light. The spiritual light lives within the fetus. When you are born and you are dunked in the clear spring water to take your first breath, you receive the gift of life, which will help you in the world of material evolution.

At the end of the day, we would go again to the front porch and watch the Sun drop down behind the trees. Grandpa would say, "It is time to deal with nature." And we would open ourselves and pray. The prayers were always those of thanksgiving.

In order to ensure solitude, one should practice visualizing a spiritual circle around himself. This process rekindles yourself and keeps an aura close around you. Everyone has an area around himself that is his own residence. Sometimes he will permit certain people he loves to enter this circle.

The early Seneca meditated very often on how best to achieve self-improvement. He made an honest study of his personal self, both good and bad. He decided what changes he wanted to make in his personal self-pattern. He listed the personal habits he wished to establish, and he listed the personal habits he wished to break.

One must always evaluate the goals which he is contemplating. Will your goals of self-improvement bring about an expansion of positive experiences?

Examine your environment. Do you control your environment, or does it control you?

Seek new dimensions of awareness by looking around you and discovering that which directly affects you.

Tap into your creative ability and raise your highest intellectual self. Discover personal techniques whereby you might better control your gifts and abilities. Raise your perception to the unlimited level of spirituality.

Your own personal symbolism can enable you to establish a focal point for meditation. If you believe that you need some kind of gimmick to aid in your self-development, don't go out and buy some tacky external thing. Discover a personal symbol that truly fits your own personality.

The ancient Senecas taught their children to pray at an early age. The children would pretend that they were in council.

They would pray in thanksgiving. This was their first introduction to going into the Silence, seeking self-development, and offering proper prayers.

The young Seneca were told to tap into their highest intellectual awareness.

They were told not to force awareness. This is a passive state that must come at its own pace.

They were instructed that prayer was a creative process that began with an idea. Prayer must be accompanied with feeling. This is so important. You cannot have prayer without having a definite idea accompanied with feeling.

They were taught that in order to have a prayer fulfilled, it is necessary to understand the levels of feeling. This understanding must exist before desires and actions can be controlled.

One of the first things Seneca children learned was that they might create their own world, their own environment, by visualizing actions and desires in prayer. A child will create his own world through imagery. He will create his own environment. This is a natural gift with which we are all born. The Senecas believed that everything that made life important came from within. Prayer assisted in developing a guideline toward discipline and self-control.

I am saddened by the fact that today's parents do not discipline their children on a very high spiritual level. This is so important, Brad.

Indeed it is, Twylah. This kind of discipline has to do with attitudinal structures, with how to instill proper values, with how best to educate the young person to grow so that the parent might at the same time continue his own growth. Twylah, might you give us an example of a proper prayer, one that might be given in the correct attitude of thanksgiving, rather than that of supplication?

TWYLAH: Yes, Brad, I would be happy to share one of my own:

O Great Spirit, I awake to another sun,
Grateful for gifts bestowed, granted one by one.
Grateful for the greatest gift, the precious breath of life.
Grateful for abilities to guide me day and night.
As I walk my chosen path of lessons I must learn,
Spiritual peace and happiness, rewards of life I learn.
Thank you for your spiritual strength, and for my thoughts
to pray;
Thank you for your infinite love that guides me through
the day.

Chief Eagle, Twylah has told us that she is often aware of the presence of her ancestor, the great chief Red Jacket. Although we have discussed your emulation of Crazy Horse's ideals, do you feel any identification with your ancestor?

CHIEF EAGLE: Yes, I do. I am descended from Crazy Horse on my mother's side. Crazy Horse was a mystic. He had the ability to go to another level of intelligence, another level of energy. He developed his mind very keenly. The Indians called him a quiet man, not a strange man, as has been so often said. The Sioux people understood these things.

My grandfather had the ability to leave his shadow. Yes, that is what I said. The Sun could be out bright, and he would just walk away from his shadow.

Yes, that is illogical. Levitation is illogical. Reading peoples' thoughts is illogical. Many things that our people take for granted are considered illogical by the dominant society.

Once when I was camping with my family in the mountains, my boy was climbing high on a teepee pole. A Medicine person named Foggy Bird came over to visit me. Just then my little boy slid down the pole onto a bed of cactus. He was screaming in pain. I asked Foggy Bird to help me.

He pulled down my boy's pants and yanked some of the needles out, but I know he didn't get them all. He spat on the boy's rump and said some prayers. Right then my boy went limp. I thought he had fainted, but Foggy Bird told me he was only sleeping.

My boy was asleep for maybe an hour and a half when we got him up. He awoke without a mark on his rump. Just before Foggy Bird started spitting and praying, I saw actual large, white lumps where the needles were. After the boy's sleep, all traces of the terrible pricks had disappeared. To this day, my son knows nothing of what happened.

I believe that one of the basic essentials in Medicine Power is a belief in a total partnership with the world of spirits and the ability to make personal contact with grandfathers and grandmothers who have changed planes of existence. In today's society, many people would feel awkward about recognizing a partnership with the Spirit World. What advice could you give to a person who might say "I can go along with vision quests, dream teachings, walking in balance on the Earth Mother, but once you are dead, you are dead. I want to follow Medicine Power, but I cannot accept a Spirit World."

TWYLAH: The first thing that I would say to such a person would be to ask him if he had ever had an experience that made him wonder if there might not be a possibility of a Spirit World. If the person were reluctant to discuss this, I would ask him if he feared death. If he did and he admitted to this fear, I would ask him just what put the fear into him. Was it religious teachings? A dread of the unknown?

In either case, I would say that fear has a great deal to do with his rejection of spirits. Immediately, the person rejected the notion of spirits on an intellectual level, but his judgment was influenced by an emotional level. When you confront the person with this, you must ask him to decide where he resides on an emotional level. Nine times out of ten, this tact opens a person up, because he must talk about this and look at it from another approach than the one with which he was familiar.

Then I might ask if he has ever thought strongly of a loved one who has passed over. Had it ever occurred to him that he may have had that strong thought because the person was close to him in spirit at that moment? I would suggest that the next time he had this sensation that he have a conversation with the person in spirit. I can promise that he will have a wonderful feeling.

Some people will open up right away and say, "Yes, I did have such an experience."

For those who have never had such an experience, or will not admit to one, I can promise a wonderful feeling if they will try it the next time they have a strong thought of someone in spirit.

You have to have a place to begin with people, and this very small, insignificant way can start the seed growing. Once a person opens up, the entities, the spirits, will come.

Everyone wants proof of survival in spirit, and so did I.

I have many times over proved the existence of the Spirit World to my own satisfaction.

Another thing, talking to others who have had experiences with spirits helps a person get over being embarrassed about such matters. If you are in a group and their vibrations are in harmony with yours, you can grow in spiritual matters and be supported by others.

The most important thing in Medicine is the importance of balancing the human being as he should be governed by the laws of nature. I don't think that to seek this balance is to turn back. If we turn toward our highest intellectual selves and begin to listen to our creative selves, we would certainly have more peace of mind.

The Indian has always known that in order to keep his peace of mind, he must keep his balance with nature. He knew that the minute he became out of balance with nature, he was going to have trouble. The moment *anyone* is out of balance with nature, *he is in trouble!*

Even if you live in a large city, you can still keep somewhat in balance with nature. You can know what foods are best for you. You can know how much sleep you need, and how you can best adjust to your individual cycles.

Yes, I think that if a person truly wants to have a peaceful life in the midst of turmoil, he can have it. But he must learn to establish a balance and to control his own thoughts, so that he can look at the material world and see it for what it really is. That world of noise and confusion is for controlling, not for wallowing.

16

the coming
great purification
and the emergent new age

As I travel about the country lecturing to groups and visiting with Medicine people and New Age visionaries, I am continually met by men and women who attempt to define a sense of urgency that has caused them to quit good jobs so that they may await they know not what. Older people as well as younger people seem haunted by a foreboding of impending, major changes which are about to transform society and humanity into something other than they presently encompass.

Some interpret these vibrations, these foreshadowings of some dramatic future event, to be the Day of Judgment which is promised in the Bible, a day in which the "elect" will be removed from the Earth and the "condemned" will be left behind to perish. Because of my own visions and those of the Medicine people and New Age prophets, I do not see this coming super-event to be the end of the world. I do believe, however, that we are entering the latest in a series of transitional periods which are necessary for mankind's spiritual evolution.

As Dallas Chief Eagle phrased it, "From the point of view of Indian theology, there is no such thing as the end of the world. There are upheavals, colossal upheavals, but no great end of the world.

"I look at the Earth Mother as a relation of mine," Chief Eagle went on. "I don't think people realize that our Mother Earth has a nervous system, just like a human body. I don't believe our fair Earth Mother can take any more of the abuse that it has been forced to suffer by man. And when the nervous system of this planet is upset, it has to readjust itself, just like any other organism. The Earth Mother has to make its own adjustments and retain its balance. And when it does this, there will be catastrophes on its surface . . . and mere man is going to suffer."

I agree with Chief Eagle and both ancient and contemporary Amerindian prophets that there will be great physical cataclysms attendant with this transitional period, this time of Great Cleansing, but I believe that they will be as nothing compared to the psychological cataclysms which will be experienced by those men and women who have not prepared themselves for the coming change in consciousness. Those people who are today ignoring the abundant cultural omens of change, those who will not restructure their methods of thought, those who will not release their hold on material reality, will be literally shattered.

As I have said in my sharings with groups throughout the United States, I fear mass suicides, incredible epidemics of nervous breakdowns among those men and women who refuse to recognize the ever-expanding, ever-widening cracks in this material dimension of being, and who resist acknowledging their sensate consensus of reality for the flimsy construct that it really is.

Hopi traditionalists are storing food and water for the coming Great Purification. They have been told that there will be a terrible famine sometime soon—no longer than two or three years in the future. Canned and dehydrated foods, seed, kerosene lamps, bottled water, and water purification tablets are being put aside in carefully concealed caches.

Sun Bear told me that his Bear Tribe is judiciously putting away stores of food and survival materials in the manner of the Hopi. "According to one of the ancient prophecies," he said, "the Great Purification will come after the whiteman has built a house in the sky. We believe that prophecy refers to Skylab."

When I asked Sun Bear if there might be anything that the System might do to stave off the approaching cleansing of the Earth Mother, he shook his head and replied:

"We know that it has already happened in the Spirit World. Soon Spirit Time will become our time, and it will happen here on Earth. There is nothing man can do to stop it. The Earth Mother will shake fleas off her back, just as a dog rids itself of its parasites. When the Cleansing has occurred, good people of spiritual awareness will build a better world."

What about all the brothers and sisters, who for one reason or another, just cannot get out of the cities to prepare for the Great Cleansing?

SUN BEAR: You are asking for kind words, and all I can say is that the reality is that they had better get their reality together and get out. I see no possible survival in the cities. The whole structuring of a city is anti-nature. Anti-nature is anti-anything that is real.

We tell the brothers and sisters that they should get everything they can together and pack their suitcases and get out. If you have to get food stamps, get all the stuff in the supermarkets you can beg off people, and hit the trail. If you have stock in the stock market, sell it and get out. If you want to put your money in something, buy wheat, not wheat futures. That way you can feed yourself at least.

The reality is that the people have to have a cleansing of themselves. The Earth Mother is going to cleanse itself. The people are going to have to cleanse themselves by getting rid of past concepts of things and by coming in harmony with the land.

It will be important to find people to whom you can relate—a group that comes together and offers harmony. But human beings have to regenerate their mental outlook so that they can come together in complete harmony.

And harmony cannot come alone from going up on a mountaintop and doing the bit of contemplating on your navel and thinking that is all there is to it. That kind of mysticism is selfish, because you are only riveting into yourself.

Go up and spend your time fasting and take in knowledge, but remember that all the great Medicine leaders of the past, leaders like Crazy Horse, were asking, "How can I best serve my people?" Unless knowledge is for some purpose, like helping you to find a better balance or helping you work together with your brothers and sisters, it doesn't mean a thing.

If you can embrace one another with a real love and a real sense of responsibility for each other, then you can really go up on the mountaintop or the Medicine lodge or the meadow and make true Medicine. You will even be able to make crops grow. That is a reality.

The old Medicine people of the Pawnee used to plant corn in the middle of winter. They would sing Medicine songs and the corn would grow up in one day. They used to prove this in front of the great American generals, who would come out and see it done. There are forces powerful enough so that if you can link up with them, they can do tremendous things.

This System is destroying itself because of the selfish pitting of people against one another. The only way we can heal people is individually. There is no way to heal this nation, because it is dead. It will be destroyed. Not by brothers wanting to take revenge on the System, but by much more powerful forces than revolution.

The only way anyone will survive the Great Purification is to cleanse himself as much as he can, so that he can function as a true brother who will live with others in harmony. This is the most important Medicine for survival. This nation is being destroyed because of the energies of hate, selfishness, and destruction that it has created. Now those energies have reversed their field and they are coming down on us.

And this destruction is too far set in motion to be halted?

It has already been sealed. The spirits that we have spoken to have said that it has already happened. It is sealed. This is a thing like we are on a continuous time belt, and we can't see tomorrow, because from our little point of view, we haven't gotten there yet. In the spiritual universe, tomorrow is already here. This is sealed and no changes can be made.

Don Wanatee says the Mesquakie, a people who have proudly maintained the old traditions, see a great catastrophe happening soon to "rearrange things":

"It will possibly be a great fire of some type, and it will leave pockets of men and women who will begin to people the Earth again. This is what the prophets of the Mesquakie have maintained. They have prophesied that the many people with their many languages will want to come back to their old religion. These people will want to return to the traditionalists to learn. There are traditional pockets in Mexico and in the United States. People here in Iowa have called us heathens, pagans. We shall see we are all brothers after all.

"I think the end might be very near. I am not speaking as a pessimist, but as one who believes in the prophecies of the Mesquakie. They prophesied great trailways in the sky. They said that the animals would be dying. They said when many species were becoming extinct, man would begin to see unusual things. Floods, earthquakes. It would be as if the Earth were revolting against its inhumane treatment.

"Other Indian tribes throughout the country are beginning to see these things coming. Many are saying in desperation, 'What can we do to revive the old tradition? How can we get back to it?' Well, there is a way for them to return, of course; but time is very short."

With the Great Purification just around the time loop, might we not expect some assistance and guidance from the Spirit World?

Twylah told me that she was certain that there were spiritual hands trying to lead the way.

"We will see more and more Indian ghosts walking across the land," Chief Eagle said. "They are coming back to touch the whiteman's heart. They are coming back not only for the Indian's sake, but for the sake of the entire globe."

Sun Bear commented, "All over this land are the guardians, or keepers, of the Earth Mother. We traditional people are the living visible guardians of this land. The others, the ghosts, are the keepers and protectors over us. There are guardian spirit forces all over the land, but there are also spirits of destruction about.

"The destroyers are all over now, too; and you can see the expression of the energies they have created. There is a violent spirit that hovers over this land like a cloud. These destroyers will soon unleash their entire strength. The only people who will retain their balance will be the people who have linked into their minds the things that are really solid and true. These people will survive because they will keep themselves away from the centers of strife and destruction. This is a headless nation now. Before too long, it will be devoured by the things it has created."

In a recent issue of *Survival*, a publication of the Church and School of Wicca in Salem, Missouri, Gavin and Yvonne Frost, Celtic traditionalists, discussed a number of prophecies relevant to the coming Earth changes:

Edgar Cayce . . . predicted in 1943 that in the next 30 or 40 years the earth will be broken up in the western portion of America. The greater portion of Japan must go into the sea. . . . Land will appear off the east coast of America. There will be a shifting of the poles. . . . The sinking or rising of the Mediterranean is given as one pointer to the start of these events.

This change in the Mediterranean area may be that mentioned in the Old Testament in several places. *Zechariah* 14, v. 4: "And his feet shall stand in that day upon the Mount of Olives . . . [which] shall cleave . . . towards the east and toward the west." V. 8: "Living waters shall go out from Jerusalem, half of them toward the former sea, and half of them toward the hinder sea."

Ezekiel had a vision of fishermen standing on the shores of the Dead Sea, harvesting great quantities of fish. At the moment, nothing will live in the waters of the Dead Sea. However, an earthquake which would split Palestine would cause the waters of the Mediterranean to flow right through to the Red Sea on the other side. The prophecy has clearly not occurred yet, and could be tied in with the Cayce forecast.

In the Writings of the Ba'hai religion, the same prophecy occurs concerning America. The Eskimos and Canadian Indians will be the future leaders of the people of this country, the Writings state.

John Pendragon, the British Seer, in his book *The Strange Life of the Man Who Sees the Future* written in collaboration with Brad Steiger, says he has seen great danger for the cities of the Atlantic Coast from Boston to Baltimore. He says this might occur in 15, 20, or more years. His book was published in 1968.

Cayce says the "safety lands" will include Ohio, Indiana,

and Illinois, much of the southern portion of Canada, and the eastern portion of Canada.

Both he and Pendragon, together with the Ba'hai Writings and the Bible Prophets, foresee great land movements and floods.

Throughout the world various men and women are becoming subject to a new dispensation of alleged spiritual communication which comes to them in the form of telepathic messages from "Space Brothers." These New Age channelers for supposed beings from other worlds or other dimensions often relay urgent messages for mankind which have to do with the coming Earth changes and the survival of those *Homo sapiens* who are of the requisite spiritual awareness. Here are certain pertinent "telethought" relays from Robin McPherson, a Space Brother channeler from Burnaby, British Columbia:

. . . a tilt will bring about the complete destruction of the Earth as it now exists in its physical sense. There will only be a handful of beings left after the tilt, and we [Space Brothers] will take them away and keep them safe. After the Earth crystallizes again, we will once again make it safe for your habitation. . . . The Earth will be totally new in every aspect.

Never fear total destruction, for it [the terrible series of cataclysms] will only be a temporary thing. It should be viewed as a series of events which will completely change the world structure.

Keep away from large cities, because the massive structures will crush your beings.

You people of Earth must pay attention to geological and geographic changes in the near future. We can no longer hold the force field as firmly as we have in the past.

If you reside in suburban areas, please let this be a warning. Do not live in midcity centers if you can avoid doing so. All over the world changes are taking place more rapidly, and your cities are becoming more and more erratic with each passing day.

The ocean floor around the Mediterranean area will be raised.

The danger in Newfoundland is similar: the country is coastal and lies near the borders of the sunken continent of Atlantis. How else could Atlantis rise again without bringing about the sinking of these coastal lands?

Newfoundland is just the starting point. The entire Eastern coast will be affected, right down to Virginia. All cities will be inundated which are in the area east of Montreal. The land mass will split south and curve into a line down to West Virginia.

I believe the coming transition will be one of change for the entire species, an evolutionary leap forward for man on both a biological and spiritual level, a move from what we now understand as humanhood to a higher consciousness in a new mode of being. For those who will raise skeptical eyebrows, I will document a change in our society's reality construct which may indicate that the period of transition has already been set in motion.

Early in September 1973, Senator Harold Hughes of Iowa announced his decision to give up a powerful position in national politics for the subsistence-level life of a religious lay worker. Just twenty years ago, Hughes had restructured his reality when he transformed himself from an alcoholic truck driver into a three-term governor and then went on, in 1968, to become a senator who would be suggested as a presidential candidate. As an active senator, Hughes was responsible for the passage of major legislation and the outspoken exposé of the secret bombings in Cambodia.

Why would the fifty-one-year-old Hughes turn his back on a promising political career that might very well have seen him in the presidency in another decade? According to Senator Hughes, "The problems of the world are more spiritual than they are legislative. Man isn't going to change just by changing laws. He must change his heart.

"Material things and power are not important in eternity. I believe we can solve international conflicts easier through a common belief in God or a creator, whether he be Christian, Muslim, Hindu or other."

While it is true that one man's decision does not an evolution make, let me go on indicating significant signs of the times.

In their July 1973 issue, *Ramparts* magazine disclosed that many of the young radicals and followers of New Left have abandoned politics in favor of the search for inner peace. Rennie Davis, formerly one of the most successful fund raisers and orators in the New Left movement, has become "blissed out" due to his treading the spiritual path indicated by a fifteen-year-old guru, Maharaj Ji.

In response to a growing demand for spiritual fulfillment, the United States is becoming the new Mecca for missionaries from the East. Eastern mysticism offers much that appeals to alienated youth who are desperately searching for a more meaningful life. In addition, the teachings of Amerindian prophets and Amerindian mystical traditions are being sought as a means of escaping the specter of an automated existence in an impersonal, technological culture. The new trip to take is "inside." The great new vistas lie within one's own spiritual depths.

These are heavy revelations to the New Leftists. Reared in a time when the behaviorist school of psychology held dominion, when the church had veered from spiritual expression to humanistic institution, these young people had been conditioned to accept life as a cause-and-effect mechanism. If the government was corrupt, you cast out the offenders. If the war was unjust, you refused to serve and you burned your draft card. If the laws concerning drugs were hypocritical, you popped pills illegally and grew your own marijuana. Such steps as these were considered "positive" actions which were supposed to comprise the cause which would bring about the desired effect—a basic change in the way of life in the United States of America.

History will record that the radical actions of the New Left did bring about many changes in the social and political structures. However, the lack of immediate response to many of the inadequacies of North American life slowly eroded the young peoples' enthusiasm for what they had envisioned as their brave, new world. Thousands of them became discouraged and joined the Establishment, which they had been attempting to change or to tear down. Others went off into what patches of wilderness remained on the continent and withdrew from the slough in which their society floundered. The behavioristic, pragmatic approach to life which they had been taught had proved unworkable when applied to the larger problems of complicated social structures and the intricate balances of power which pervade the human existence. The false reality of direct-action solutions to human problems was found wanting by thousands of young activists. What had appeared to be sharply defined, obvious problem areas were found to have long, gray shadows which were not visible from the viewpoint of pure, materialistic idealism.

But while this sociological phenomenon had been swelling and peaking, an equally profound cultural development had been in progress. Enormous populations of school-age youth had turned on to drugs; and North American society was totally unprepared to cope with the kids' attraction to marijuana, LSD, "speed," and all the other consciousness-raising, psyche-altering, mood-changing chemicals.

This combination of political activism and drug indulgence turned millions of parents away from their own children. The lines of demarcation were drawn. A counter-culture was born and was forced to live outside the societal stockade. Just as a community of poor Americans exists scant yards from the cornucopia of material abundance, so now did a new community of spiritually disenfranchised American youth live in its own ghettos. Their reality had become a reality separate from that of their parents.

But with the disillusionment of activist New Left movements and the exposure of the drug trip as a passport to a false and sinister shadowland, millions of young people—together with more of their older brothers and sisters and parents than has been realized—began to turn constructively inward. The influence of New Age mystics and Amerindian Medicine people surfaced in music, hair styles, and fashions, and the media began to focus on the "Age of Aquarius," an approaching time of transition.

Our new generation of mystics are very reluctant to commit themselves to any "ism" that offers selective salvation and a single path to life eternal. The majority of them have opted for universalism and a spirituality that belongs to everyone.

Today there are groups of metaphysicians and men and women hoping to retribalize in traditional Amerindian style in nearly every community in North America. The majority of them are interested only in concentrating on self-awareness and in promoting true brotherhood. An entire generation has structured a new and vital reality for themselves. They will be prepared for the coming period of transition.

In his book *Uni-Chotometrics*, Eugene A. Albright describes his vision of the impending change, the Tomorrow which has been variously described and named throughout history as the New Age, the Advent of the New Man, the Millennium, the Great Purification.

Albright writes, "The next . . . evolving technique of the human organism, will be the opening up of two specific functions which, up to this stage of development, have been latent.

"One of these is the capacity to control the environment completely; to cause matter in the environment to disintegrate and restructuralize directly on an energy level. The other is to structure the function of the body and replenish it without necessity for food, either plant or animal life."

Albright expresses his opinion that in the past there have been periods in which the vibratory rate was stepped up. "Many who cannot adjust to higher rates of vibration are destroyed," he says. "This may appear to be cruel, but nature and that which is natural, has always prevailed and it will prevail."

In my book *Revelation: The Divine Fire*, I deal with contemporary prophets and revelators, men and women such as the Medicine people, who claim communication with Higher Intelligence. In my opinion, throughout history and in all lands, the revelatory experience has been designed to inform mankind of certain universal precepts.

1. There is a Higher Intelligence, or Energy Source, from which every man might draw power and inspiration.

2. Man has within him all that is necessary to establish harmony with Higher Intelligence, provided certain spiritual conditions are encouraged and maintained.

3. Man is one with all other men in spirit and has a sense of unity with all things. Man's soul is both universal and individual.

4. Man is evolving toward a New Age, that is, a dramatic progression in his evolution as a spiritual being. We are moving toward a state of mystical consciousness wherein every man shall be a god under God.

It is my belief that the central purpose of the revelatory process throughout history has been to lead *Homo sapiens* to the understanding that he can be so much more than a creature of conditioned reflexes, biochemical compounds, and glandular responses and that he is evolving as a spiritual being and progressing out of his old, physical limitations into a higher consciousness that is his by right of his cosmic inheritance.

The greatest lesson that the Medicine people—together with all the inspired men and women of history—have shared from their perspective of heightened consciousness has been that material, consensual reality is subject to dramatic change by the essential self of each individual. Each man and woman has the latent ability to shape a reality separate from that of the ordinary and the commonly accepted.

When one has absorbed this basic lesson and discovered his own techniques for application, his own Medicine, he has truly learned how to survive the coming time of Great Purification and how to hasten his own spiritual evolution.

P51